It's My Story So I'll Tell It

To the people who assisted with this project: Thank you so much for your input and understanding. It's not easy to involve yourself in another person's dream and help bring their story to life, but you did. Whereas my story is unique to me, many can relate to much of my life as a child and as an adult. Without you, this would not have been possible. I am forever grateful.

To my loving soulmate who thought she knew all there was to know: I have been blessed by your patience. Because you accepted me as I was and never stopped believing, I'm a lucky man.

To our children who created many challenges that parents face raising kids: Rochanda (Shon), Dwayne, and Tiffany, my love for you goes deeper than you could ever imagine.

My inspiration for this project grew out of a desire to impart some knowledge of my family's origin and highlight some of their struggles. After many hours of research and conversations with elders still living, I've learned so much about our family that I didn't know. There is so much about the struggles our forefathers endured on a path to a better life that was never discussed or documented. Those who lived the struggle are no longer here, so a complete history can never be known.

I thought I could capture my life story in short order. I quickly realized, as I looked back in time, there is so much about a particular occasion I took for granted at the time. As I recalled past events, I wondered how I survived many of the situations I was involved with, but now I realize everything that occurred was the ingredients that went into developing the person I became. Sharing with my kids a snapshot of our forefathers' early history and how life for me as a child, young adult, and throughout the subsequent years will show that a person born into challenging times can excel. Having a desire to work for what you want and to never stop striving for better is all that's required. Disappointments are part of the process one must use as learning tools for growth. Mistakes are also a part of the equation. They, too, are learning tools. All it takes is your relationship with God, effort on your part, and never accepting "just okay."

Table Of Content

Chapter One

The Family's Foundation

My story began on the 8th day of May, the year 1953. On that day, a baby boy was born to Mr. and Mrs. O.C. and Lois Marsh and given Nelson as his name. Before me, my parents had two kids, Rose (Sister) and a boy they named James (JT). Sadly, prior to JT, another child was born but did not survive. I don't recall much from my birth to about age three or four, so much of what is known about those years was told to me. As recorded in Washington County records, my birth record indicates I was delivered by a midwife, Mary Robinson, who was commonly known as Mae Tite throughout the community. Back then, most births in the country were handled by an attending midwife who would travel by wagons pulled by mules. Oftentimes, when the midwife made it to town to have the birth recorded, she had forgotten what the child was to be named, which explains how many got their name as the midwife, having attended to several births, reported what she thought the parents told her what the name should be. My birth was recorded forty-five days later.

The "country," as I and many others know it to be, is Washington-on-the-Bluff. It's located not far from Washington-on-the-Brazos State Park, and, as Texas history was taught back then, we learned this was the site where Texas declared its independence from Mexico and signed its Declaration of Independence. Washington-on-the-Brazos briefly served as the Capital of Texas and is recorded as the birthplace of Texas. Many of the men responsible for developing the community were freed slaves or their offspring.

One member of the group, Mr. Eugene Laster, had a conversation with his daughter-in-law, Mrs. Ella Whiting Laster (1893–1971), where he reported being brought to Texas from Morgan County, Georgia, when he was about seven years of age during the year 1859. Without having any records or knowledge as to why, one can opine with this being a period just before the signing of the Emancipation Proclamation and him being the male child born to a slave woman, he could have been sold to another enslaver in Texas.

History teaches that a male child born to a slave woman sired by a white master could not remain on the plantation and would be sold. I often wondered why Mama's mother, Essie Laster,

had a picture of a man hanging on the wall above the fireplace. I later learned he was my great-grandfather. The picture was one of her father, Mr. Eugene Laster[1]. The conversation between Ella and Eugene Laster was said to have occurred sometime during the 1930s and is the first known report of what became the community of Washington-on-the-Bluff. He indicated that at age nineteen, he married Julia Fielder in 1871, and they had fifteen children together. Ms. Essie Laster (1899-1991) was one of the fifteen and was my mother's mother.

According to Eugene Laster, other men freed by the Emancipation Proclamation and left various plantations settled in Washington County. Several gathered one day in 1880 to discuss the needs of their community. According to that conversation, as recorded by his daughter-in-law, he and the five other Black men at that meeting discussed the desire for the community to have a place of worship and a place for their kids to learn to read and write. They wanted their family members to be taught God's words and for their kids to attend school. They knew their forefathers, and many of them had endured years of slavery, and the only thing that brought them thus far was their unwavering faith in God. At that gathering, they pooled together about sixty dollars and agreed to work for a white landowner for a few days in return for seventeen dollars and two acres of land.

Many could not read or write but believed the only way to survive in a white society was to serve God, who was essential in their lives, and book learning for their kids. In 1882, they selected land south of the Brazos River, high on a bluff, and built a shed-like building they named St. Matthews Baptist Church. They needed land for a cemetery, so they purchased three additional acres from another white landowner in January 1884. The first church building (shed) served the community until it became too small, so a larger building was erected in the early 1900s and used until a storm in 1915 destroyed the building.

Following the 1915 storm, the church was rebuilt, but the cornerstone wasn't placed until 1935. Even though the church had many setbacks, the determination of its founding members established the foundation for a place of worship that stands to date. A school, which was a large one-room building, was built nearby and called St. Matthews Elementary School. No records for the date it was built could be found, and the school shut down in the mid-1960s. I remember the church with the 1935 cornerstone sitting among stately live oak trees

with a tall steeple housing a large bell. The bell would toll each time one of the residents in the community passed, and as kids, we would count the number of times the bell tolled, thinking the number indicated the person's age at passing. The church was rebuilt in 1965, and the most recent renovations were completed in 2009.

Growing up in a country environment, all the kids knew they had to help work the fields, do chores around the house, and stay out of grown folks' business. You were expected to stay in a child's place; if you didn't, you got a backhand across your lips. The man was the head of the house, and what he did or said was never questioned. The wife and the kids lived and were raised in a house where the father was a strong and controlling figure, and they feared what would happen if his manhood was challenged. The children were never privy to conversations between adults and never saw any troubles within the marriage. Inasmuch, they were unaware of or could recognize spousal abuse if it occurred.

In many cases, the young girls saw marriage at an early age as a way to escape the wrath of a mean father, only to find they had united with a male whose example of a father did not know any other way. I now better understand why the women of that era were submissive to the men. We know conduct acceptable in that era is no longer tolerated today.

The elders worked the land and had many kids to help work the fields, put food on the table, and still went to church on Sundays. It was hard to scratch out a living just to survive, but somehow, they still found time to sneak and creep. Mama and Daddy already had Sister, born September 19, 1946, before they married. After getting married, they went to live with his mother, Ms. Aquila Avery.

We called her Grandma. They lived on property owned by a white man named Mr. Yeager and worked in his fields for the privilege of having somewhere to live, earning a dollar a day. My brother, JT, was born June 26, 1950, but trouble between Mama and Daddy resulted in her leaving six weeks after JT was born, walking back to her parents' house with Sister in tow. She didn't stay away long and went back to Daddy. She had me in 1953 while there with his mother. My siblings said they never saw our daddy's father, and Grandma didn't discuss him. Later, it was learned his name was James Marsh,

but everyone called him "Sunchie." No one seemed to know what happened to him, only to say he left one day and never returned. Our daddy was brought up on Mr. Yeager's farm and, when he was old enough, helped work in the fields. Those who worked as sharecroppers never yield much more than another back-breaking year of hard work with nothing to show.

The land owner got the proceeds from that year's crop, and nothing was left for the sharecropper. History reveals that all they had was hope that the next year would be the year they wouldn't hear,

"Well, you almost made enough to pay for the seeds, the groceries, and supplies you got on credit. Maybe you will make a better crop next year and have enough to pay off your debt. Don't worry. You always have a home here."

Some of the men left the farm in search of a better job to support a family, while others gave up and deserted their families, leaving the women and kids to make it on their own. Now that Daddy had a family to support, he left us with his mother and went to Houston, seeking a better-paying job. I gather he realized there was no future in working on the farm and had heard of better opportunities in the city. I'm told I was about six months old when he left with the intention of getting settled and returning for his family.

We continued to live with Grandma while Sister watched JT and me as Mama and Grandma worked in the fields and kept house.

I don't remember seeing Daddy much during my baby years, but I was told he would sometimes visit. My memory of Grandma in those early days is also limited because we didn't stay too long after Daddy left. Mama eventually had to move back in with her parents, Mr. and Mrs. Travis (1896-1975) and Essie Laster Bennett (1899-1991)

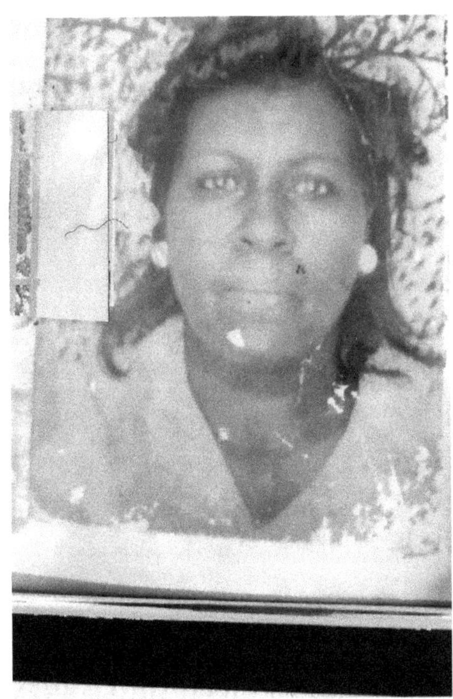

because the little money made from working in the fields wasn't enough to take care of two adults and three kids, and Daddy wasn't sending any money home. Mama would take us to visit Grandma on occasion, and we would spend the night. She snored so loudly at night that I thought a wild animal was in the house. My first real memory of the man Mama said was my daddy. I was around three years old and still living with Mama's parents. We called them Big Mama and Big Daddy. When Daddy would come over, Mama would look and see him coming and send us out to meet him. She would say, "Here come y'all daddy. Go see him." He would rub our heads and ask, "Where's your mama?"

I don't remember ever going hungry, being without clothes, or having shelter, but believe me, we were poor! Mama was one of nine kids born to her parents, and her daddy farmed a small parcel of land. He raised cotton and did a lot of hunting. He made extra money selling fish he caught out of the Brazos River, and the word was that he cooked and sold sour mash. That was until the revenue men showed up and took him away. I don't think he did it anymore after he got back. Most of their kids (Irene, James, Berthenia, Bernice, Tommie, Florence, Lois, Dora, and Blanche) received some schooling and, when old enough, left home. Uncle James was drafted into the army and settled in San Francisco when he got out. Aunties Berthenia and Blanche later married and eventually moved to San Francisco. Aunt Bernice died during childbirth, leaving a daughter to be reared by Aunt Berthenia. Aunt Florence married and moved with her husband to Detroit, where he got work in the motor car industry. Uncle Tommie left for Houston and made his living with a deck of cards. He never had a real job or a social security card but did well as a professional gambler.

Mama,

Aunties Irene (Aunt Sang), and Dora all married and stayed in the country. Mama Lois was born February 26, 1926; folks called her "Twenty-six." With her meager upbringing and schooling, she learned what was then called the three R's: reading, 'riting, and 'rithmetic. I never asked Mama what grade level she completed, but she read, could write well, and did figuring. Additionally, she had a wealth of common sense. The old folks called it "mother wit." In most houses, the only book in the home was a Bible, so I guess Big Mama read to her kids, so Mama read to us. We were made to learn scripture from the Bible and were expected to say it after Mama finished praying. Mama learned the skills necessary to care for a family from watching her mother and other elders in the community and probably from the School of Hard Knocks.

Folks back then worked the land, raised a garden, and took from nature the things they needed to put food on the table. Everyone in the community was always available to offer a helping hand, extend a handout, or hand down to those in need. We received clothes that were passed down when they no longer fit or if someone got fortunate enough to get new clothes.

The biggest event during the year was at hog-killing time. Neighboring men and their wives would gather at the home of the person with hogs ready for slaughter. The men butchered and prepared the meat to be placed in a smokehouse, cooked the hog cracklings, and made lard. The women cleaned the chitlings and casing for making sausage. The kids were expected to stay away from grownup conversations and waited for the cracklings to get done but had the chore of keeping the fire hot under the black washpot. Everybody pitched in and went home with fresh hog meat and a bag of hog cracklings. The whole day was set aside for hog killing and visiting with people they wouldn't get to see often. That's probably when the sneaking and creeping was arranged for the many rendezvous where they met their lover behind the crib or in the woods.

Everyone in the family worked in the fields and didn't frown on hard work. Hard work was passed down from their ancestors because they knew if they didn't work, they didn't eat. What anchored everyone was the firm belief that nothing was impossible with God on their side. When the work week was done, they spent Sundays giving thanks and praising God at the church on the bluff.

The children were made to attend and sat near the front of the church. You better not act up because one of the old sisters would wring your ear or thump you upside your head. The elders sheltered the kids because even though they were free, terrible things still happened to Black folks. Mama would tell us,

"Don't be looking at them white folks and stay in your place."

She furthered that by sharing a story that had been told to her of a fair-looking Black lad who had left the country for the city. He came back one weekend to visit his people. He made the mistake of having a light-skinned lady (who could pass for white) with him in a car he had bought. Back then, Black folks used mules and wagons to move around. Imagine him driving a car when most whites didn't have one! Here was this darkie, riding around with what they thought was a white woman—he had to be put in his place! He was stopped at night along one of the dark country roads, dragged from his car, and beaten to death. When he was found, his genitals had been mutilated and stuck in his mouth. No one was ever charged with what happened to him, but it was easy to figure out who and why he was killed. Mama didn't say if she knew what happened to the woman, but if she wasn't abused and managed to survive, I bet she left in a hurry and never returned. Needless to say, the story was anecdotal, but it served its purpose and scared the dickens out of me because I didn't want my tools cut off!

Believe it or not, we really didn't see a lot of white people. We had no idea what the world outside the country was like because our community was all we knew. When I did get to go to the store—owned by a big-belly white man—where most of the country folks traded, I saw the signs that said Colored Men and Colored Women painted on outdoor toilets located behind the store. A water faucet stood outside the store with a sign displaying Colored. I also would see the Black men and women always greeting the white people as Mr. or Miss So-and-So, and the men would remove their hats. They would always respond to them with a "yes sir" or "no sir" and "yes ma'am" or "no ma'am." I thought this was the way it was. I was so excited to be out that I wasn't concerned about what grown folk did; I just wished for and hoped to get a piece of candy. Normal for us didn't include things like cars, televisions, cities, tall buildings, running water, indoor restrooms, and electricity. WE WERE POOR!

Chapter Two

Tough Times

With Daddy gone and Mama not having a permanent place to live, no source of income, and having to care for three kids, how we made it can only be explained by using one word: God! If it wasn't for Big Daddy and Big Mama's help, we would have been homeless. That's why I now understand why Mama always prayed to God to grant her the strength to carry on and protect her little family. She would ask God to allow her life on earth long enough to see her children become adults. She would end every prayer with,

"Father, when I reach that Jordan River, cross me over so I might hear you say well done."

She believed in God, and He made ways for her. There is no other explanation.

Life as a child for me was simple. All I had to do was to get up each day to a plate of syrup and bread—sometimes a piece of salted bacon—red beans and cornbread for dinner and some milk and bread for supper. On occasion,

Sunday meals were different. Mama would fry a chicken if there was a young chicken in the yard ready to be plucked. Each member of my family had an assigned chicken part. Mama would have the back and a thigh; Sister and JT each got a wing and would split the breast. I got a drumstick. The neck, feet, and chicken's head were added to the gravy that was served over rice.

I didn't miss too many days without getting my behind whipped for something. I thought it was funny to put dirt in my hair just after Mama washed and combed it. When I got big enough, JT and I amused ourselves by chasing road lizards across rocky outcrops and throwing rocks at wasp nests. Knowing if we got stung by the wasp, we got our behinds whipped.

Sister, a mama-in-training, could always be found helping Mama in the house. As I got older, I, too, had to help with things around the house. Growing up sucks! We packed water from a spring where the coolest water bubbled up from the ground. Almost daily, we walked to what was commonly called the "spring branch" to get water for cooking and drinking. Water for washing and bathing was caught in a wooden barrel as it ran off the roof when it rained. Mama would wash clothes in a black washpot that we placed wood around to boil the clothes. There was no Clorox then; Mama used bluing in the washpot and lye soap made from hog lard with a scrub board to clean the clothes. The clothes were then hung on a clothesline with clothespins to dry. There was no washer or dryer back then, but no matter how poor, we were taught cleanliness is next to godliness. We never got into bed without washing up, and at bath time, we used a number two tub to take baths. The next person in line used the same water the person before you used, and when you got out of bed the next morning, you better never get caught back in it after you got up!

Meanwhile, Daddy would pop in and out enough to father another child: my brother Orange (Jr.) in 1956. Remember I told you the midwife reported what she thought the baby was to be named? Maybe Jr. should have been named Owen. Now Mama and four children were living with Big Mama and Big Daddy. Friction between Big Mama and Mama often occurred because she would get on Mama for continuing to have children knowing Daddy wouldn't take care of them. Mama's siblings, who left and settled in California, realized she would never quit seeing Daddy and having babies. They sent Mama enough money to buy tickets to go there. They thought that if they got her away from him, she would do better; that she would see the potential away from him, find work, and send for her other kids. They would provide a place for her to stay until she settled. Mama got the tickets, packed for the trip, and gathered her new baby, and Mama, Jr., and I boarded a train out of Brenham, Texas, for San Francisco, California, while Sister and JT were sent back to stay with Grandma Aquila.

The train trip took several days, going up and around mountains, finally arriving in Oakland, California. I don't recall who picked us up, but they drove us to the Hunter's Point addition, where her siblings lived. The train ride and the time in a big city was a lot for a little country boy to understand. Her siblings had cars, and everywhere there were people, buildings, and sounds unheard of by a four-year-old. And there was a big pond with large boats anchored with people moving around like ants. Many of the people looked different from the folks I was used to. Hunter's Point was where most Blacks settled after arriving in San Francisco, but there were Chinese and White Americans. Our stay in Frisco was brief because Mama could not be convinced to stay. I believe we may have stayed about three—maybe four months—at most. Mama's excuse was that she had to go back to see about the kids she had left behind. Her sister and brother told her they would help send for her other two as she settled, but nope! Mama had to go home. I believe Daddy may have had something to do with her decision.

After giving up on so many opportunities, we returned to nothing and, again, moved back with Mama's parents. Oh well! There went my opportunity to grow up in Cali. Our stay with them didn't last long because Big Mama and Mama were having very heated arguments about Mama still diddling and dabbling with Daddy. This may have been the straw that broke the camel's back. Mama moved out, and we stayed with Aunt Sang and her family for a while before Mama took us and moved into a house owned by a person Mama called Aunt Mae. We didn't live there long before Mama took us from there to live in Grandma Nancy's house,

who had passed on. Grandma Nancy was Big Daddy's mother, and guess what! Daddy would pop in, and before long, Mama had another child: my sister Irene, who was born in 1958. We lived there for several years because another baby was born after Irene but only lived for a few hours. Mama's siblings in California convinced their parents to move there so Big Daddy could work on a real job long enough to qualify for a better Social Security retirement. With them gone, we moved back to Big Mama's house and lived there while they were in San Francisco. When they returned some years later, we moved again. This time, it was to another relative's house, whom Mama called Uncle Lodges. His house was located just down the hill from Big Mama's house. It had four rooms with a wood-burning heater and a bed in the first room. The kitchen area had a wood-burning stove and table. One other room had two beds, and the last room was used as a pantry. There was no electricity, so we used kerosene lamps. We had beds to sleep on, a few chairs, and an outdoor toilet out back. Her uncle left an icebox, but Mama never had money to buy block ice to put in it. Any other items we had were gifts to Mama by others to help her keep house. Thank God for the community, for they made sure those in need had what they needed. Most of the menfolk extended a helping hand by bringing Mama stuff so we had food, clothes, and firewood. Those who weren't related probably pitched in with some sneaking and creeping in mind. If there was hanky-panky occurring, I never saw it.

As a little fellow, my job was to gather wood chips to start the fire. With JT being older, he had to ensure we had cut wood for the stove and heater. As with most little girls, Sister helped around the house and watched the little ones. Jr. was too little to help out, and Irene was a baby. As I grew older, I thought I was a man when I was allowed to use an ax to help cut the wood. The old folks showed you how because they knew the dangers associated with cutting wood. We would gather every edible food source in the woods, and Mama would preserve things like peaches, pears, and figs. She made jelly from the plums and grapes we picked. These items helped to put food on the table. Almost every house has a garden, so people would welcome you to take greens, peas, okra, or whatever they had ready. I remember Mama having a few chickens in the yard, so there were eggs when the hens were laying. A lot of times, a couple of jelly biscuits and maybe a piece of salt pork was all we had for breakfast. Mostly, we had syrup and homemade biscuits for breakfast, and if we didn't eat all the cracklings, Mama would make crackling bread.

When school started, Sister and JT would walk to the one-room school Mama Lois attended. Each day after school, they finished whatever tasks they had to do around the house and then studied for the next day. I would sit and watch Sister and JT do their homework assignments as a kerosene lamp provided light. With Mama and my siblings' help, I already knew the alphabet, could count to one hundred, and read the book about Dick, Jane, and Spot before I started school. I couldn't wait to go to school! And I guess they were my kindergarten teachers.

When the 1960 school year started, I walked with them to the same one-room schoolhouse Mama had gone to. Each day, Mama would prepare a couple jelly biscuits or egg sandwiches for our lunch using an empty syrup bucket as a lunch pail. Remember the fellow Eugene Laster who had the conversation with his daughter-in-law, Ella Laster? She grew up in Washington County, and after finishing grade school, she attended Prairie View A & M University, obtaining a bachelor's and master's degrees .

When I started school, she still taught grades one through eight at the one-room school built by the founding fathers and, in total, taught there for 52 years. During my first year in school, I completed the course studies for grades one and two that first year. I didn't think much about why our books had other kids' names written in the assigned column. I was just glad to have a book! I later learned the books were first used by the white kids and then passed down to us. This, too, was the way it was, but it didn't bother me. I was too busy enjoying the fuss the girls made over me! I guess I had it back then…I just didn't know what "it" was.

Our humble beginning and the values instilled in all the children, both in school and church, were the foundation many built their lives on and still carry to this day. On Sunday mornings, after some syrup and biscuits, Mama would see that we had our church clothes and shoes on, and off we went walking to the church on the hill for Sunday school. Church services were every other Sunday, and we would line up like little chickens following the mama hen. No matter the weather conditions, we went to church, and after we returned home, we got out of our church clothes.

It's amazing how folks with little to no education had such foresight back then. They accomplished amazing things with their limited education and belief in God, prayer, hard work, and insight into the future. They were simple people but had lots of wisdom and carried themselves in a manner that demanded respect. They would say things like,

Don't put all your eggs in one basket.

Don't get too big for your britches.

Boy, you beginning to smell your piss.

Don't burn your bridges.

Make hay while the weather is good, and put something up for a rainy day.

Don't go jump in the river 'cause so and so did it; you can't swim,

Every tub gotta set on its own bottom.

And, for the sake of your backside, they would tell you,

Boy, don't lie to me.

From past experiences, they knew to tell you,

Leave them white folks alone and stay in your place.

They made it clear to ask for what you wanted and never put your hands on anything that didn't belong to you. If you acted like you didn't want to do what they told you, they would ask, You call yourself sulking? then knock a knot upside your head with whatever they got a hand on.

A person would have to have lived a while to understand what was meant by the saying every dog got a day. I still haven't figured out what they meant by a crowing hen and a whistling woman both meet a bad end.

Mama learned well, for she kept us in line with a strap made from old leather wagon reins. Big Daddy made the strap and gave it to her with instructions to "whoop them children behind." I got my share because I was a bad little booger. I often reflect upon those days and appreciate how I was raised and from where I came. The stuff they did and said made little sense then, but now it's as real as the nose on my face.

As an adult and parent, I totally understand. Looking back, Mama had nothing but love for her children, but she would put them wagon reins on our backside if we acted up! Through all the hard times, she never stopped believing that God would make a way. She did her best to keep us clothed, fed, and a roof overhead but never let us know how tough times were. I never heard her complain. You know, I can't remember ever hearing her say anything bad about our daddy, either. She simply said, "that's your daddy," but there had to be something no one else could see because she gave that booger seven children in total! Remember, he left when I was around six months old and never did get around to coming back for us.

Chapter Three

A New Beginning

Mama finally divorced the person I knew as my daddy and later married Warren G. Byrd in 1962. We called Mama's new husband GG. I was eight when he married Mama and took us to live with him in Brazos County, where he worked on a ranch. He stepped in and took on the role of a father. Sister, who was to attend eleventh grade, went to live with Mama's sister, Aunt Dora, and her family in Brenham, Texas, where she attended Pickard High School. After she went to Brenham, we didn't see her much. When she graduated in 1964, she only came to stay with us briefly before leaving for Houston.

After Mama and GG had been married a while, another addition to the family soon came—a baby girl they named Connie. GG, like all the other folks in the country, gave everybody a nickname. For whatever reason, he nicknamed JT Big Baby; I was Minnow; Jr. became Doper, and Irene was Gomer. When Connie was born, he called her Dit. We didn't mind the nicknames because it looked like Mama had married someone nothing like our daddy this time.

We still had many tough times, but life was a whole lot better. We now lived in a house where a light bulb lit up when you flipped a switch. We used to have kerosene lamps to light a room. And now Mama didn't have to cook on a wood stove; she had to learn how to use a gas range. We still had to cut wood for the heater to keep warm during the winter months. To be living on a working cattle ranch, having a chance to learn about horses and cattle, play cowboy, and see the things associated with ranching, I was doing alright. Although so much better, we were still treated as second-class citizens because, as I think back, the house we moved into was initially intended to be a barn. The owner, realizing he needed a place for the Black help to live, had a barn, a twenty-four-by-twenty-four metal building partitioned off to make four rooms with walls and electrical service. The restroom was built out back with water supplied to the bathtub and commode. There was no hot water because there was no hot water heater. If we wanted hot water, it was heated on the stove and carried out to the tub. Water was plumbed to the restroom but not to the house. The water supply line stood just outside the back door of the house with a faucet where we got water for drinking and cooking. I always wondered why it wasn't plumbed inside the house.

We fell in love with our new place and occupied ourselves with all there was to do. There was another nice house on the ranch, just up the hill, surrounded by a chain link fence with all the amenities. No one lived there, but it was too good for Black folks. If a white family worked on the ranch, they could live there. Racial bias in plain sight! Having been sheltered from racial biases, we never thought we were discriminated against. This was just the way it was. Our parents didn't talk about those things around us and sheltered us from what was racism. Then again, they probably didn't know they were being discriminated against.

When the 1963 school year started, JT and I were enrolled at AMT Elementary School located in the community of Cawthorn. The school was a multi-room building with about seventy-three kids and seven teachers. JT and I got to ride a bus to school. Remember, we used to walk to a school where there were probably about twenty kids enrolled in total.

Needless to say, riding a school bus was exciting, but entering a school with so many kids I had never seen before was scary. I knew all the kids that went to St. Matthews. After an adjustment period, I made new friends during recess and lunch and played on swing sets and seesaws. I started there beginning in the fifth grade and excelled in most courses. My desire to learn about everything those kids knew motivated me, for there were some smart kids in my classes, and I felt I was just as good. I even got a girlfriend during my seventh-grade year, but it didn't last long because an older guy took her from me. It was just puppy love, anyway.

At the end of each school year, all the kids were loaded onto buses and taken to Washington-on-the-Brazos State Park for a school picnic.

There, the kids would spend the day exploring the park, playing games, and having a picnic lunch, all under the watchful eyes of the teachers. The park's museum offered an opportunity to learn about the history of early Texas. There are several buildings and homes of early pioneers for one to tour, but I believe we were looking for a place to smooch.

There were many great memories of my time at AMT Elementary, for school was easy for me. My most vivid memories of my time at AMT Elementary were my first day and the day the report circulated throughout the school that President Kennedy had been shot while visiting Dallas. That day, November 22, 1963, and the surrounding events will forever be etched in history and the minds of many. I didn't grasp the magnitude of what had happened at the time because neither the presidency nor who occupied the White House was discussed in our house. I don't remember talking about it after we got home that evening. I did, however, wonder why all the female teachers were crying.

Not long after we moved, Mama found a place of worship and joined Bethel Grove Baptist Church in Cawthorn, so we had to attend. Back then, churches would have a week-long nightly revival each year consisting of singing, praying, and preaching. Those not yet committed to Jesus as their savior would sit on the first row called the "mourning bench." The old folks would say, "moanin' bench." Mama made me sit on the mourning bench during one revival, and I don't know if I got that "old-time religion," but something made me get up and take the preacher's hand. Not long after, I was baptized in a farm pond not far from the church.

The ranch where we lived covered many acres with lots of woods to hunt and lakes filled with fish. During most summer weekends, JT and I would go hunting with a .22 rifle Big Daddy gave him if we had bullets for the gun. It worked fine, and we got to be pretty good with it. Hunting was another way we helped to put food on the table. If you've never had to do this, don't knock it; sometimes, that's all we had. If you ever try smothered squirrel or rabbit with 30-weight gravy over rice, you will be pleasantly surprised. Not to mention some hot, just-out-the-grease freshwater catfish browned to perfection! Who needs a steak?

When we weren't hunting or fishing, we could be found playing in a large water trough that the cows drank from. That was our swimming pool. As with most ranches, you will find barns to store hay. When they are empty, pigeons would flock there. We would chase the pigeons from one barn to the next, throwing rocks at them. We never intended to eat the pigeon because Mama wouldn't cook it. Instead, it was something to do to help pass the day. Being a working cattle ranch, it had hundreds of cattle and several horses. Being older, JT got to work during the summer on the ranch when he was around twelve.

He would receive $27.50 per week for performing the same tasks the other workers did. He thought he was grown then. He even saved up enough to buy a bicycle. After working half days on Saturdays, he would leave on his bike, so Jr. and I spent our time playing with toys I made and swimming in the water trough. Back then, I admired the equipment they used on the ranch, so I made toys to play with out of wire that resembled the same.

After a few years, GG gave me a pony and a hand-me-down saddle. I named my pony Ribbon. I spent a lot of time riding Ribbon, pretending to be a cowboy, and acting out what I saw GG and the other workers do. After working all week, GG would help other folks with animals ready to go to the auction barn on Saturdays. We would help. This was another way he earned a few more dollars to help support the family. On Sunday, we went to church.

The animals still had to be fed during the winter months, so the ranch owner grew acres of hay during the growing season. When the hay was cut and baled, we'd haul and place them in the barns. Some of the bales weighed more than us because I didn't weigh any more than 95 pounds, soaking wet! JT didn't weigh much more. Hauling hay always took place during the summer, so we would start the morning in the hay field. When GG got off, he joined us, and we would work late into the night hauling hay. While working in the hay field, I learned to drive his 1950 Chevrolet truck with a four-speed shift in the floor. The first gear was typically called the "grandma gear," so GG taught us to put it in grandma, and off it would go, creeping through the hay field. I believe the owner paid about two cents per bale to haul and place the bales in the barn.

When pecans began to fall, we would gather them to sell so GG and Mama could have money to buy stuff for Christmas. I remember well one cold day in November, GG, JT, and I went to gather pecans along a slough. GG had saddled his old mare called Tootsie, and the three of us rode to where we were to gather pecans. We were doing pretty well where we were, but for whatever reason, GG decided he wanted to cross the slough to gather pecans. The slough wasn't that deep, but, at that time, it had a thin sheet of ice along the edges. GG figured the horse would step on and break the ice. He and JT started to cross first. The horse stepped and broke the ice on the near side but decided to jump the other edge, lost her footing, fell, and down went GG, JT, and the horse into the cold water! All three made it out, and they went galloping to the house. Thank God I didn't go first. I almost busted a gut laughing as I walked home! When I got there, they were still sitting by the wood heater, trying to get warm. You see, sometimes it pays to be second. I believe that was the Christmas GG bought our first television with some of the money we got for picking up pecans. Every Christmas, no matter what, GG and Mama would always make sure each of us received a bag containing an apple, orange, holiday nuts, ribbon candy, a pack of firecrackers, sparklers, and a toy to play with.

After we got the television, we watched shows like Gomer Pyle USMC, Green Acres, Hee Haw, and Gilligan's Island. Mama fell in love with

General Hospital. We only had three channels back then, so we watched what was on. At the time, the Dallas Cowboys were the only team shown on the channels that we got, so we couldn't wait to watch them play. After the football game, we would go outside and replay the game, pretending to be one of the Dallas Cowboys. We used an old doll head as our football, and Irene would be the quarterback. I pretended to be Bob Lilly, and Jr. would be Jethro Pugh. Jr wouldn't block for Irene when he had the ball, so she got tired of getting hit and quit.

Chapter Four

The Realities of Real Life

JT left AMT after graduating the eighth grade and started ninth grade at George Washington Carver High School in Navasota, Texas. Navasota wasn't a large town, but it was the biggest town I had seen. The town's tumultuous history was often compared to Dodge City during the late 1800s and early 1900s. From 1908 until 1911, the legendary Frank Hamer was hired as the city marshal to tame the town. If a person got unruly or caught outside the law, he would kick them all the way to jail. Stories were told about the local plantation owners, the Moore brothers, who owned and farmed many acres of cotton along the Brazos River Valley. They used Blacks who could not pay their fines after being kicked to jail or from prisoners paroled to the farm from the penal system. The most notable brother was Tom Moore, who ran his plantation the same as early-day plantation owners. If a Black person got unruly on the plantation, they got whipped or killed. If a Black person came up missing or killed, his motto was, "if a mule dies, I'll buy another; if a nigger dies, I'll go get another." Once paroled to the farm, the person could never leave. There were men who had been paroled to the farm and were still working there when we moved to Brazos County in 1962. Whatever happened in Navasota, the Moore Brothers had a lot of influence.

I graduated the eighth grade at AMT in 1966, then went to Carver High School for ninth grade. This was another life-changing moment. I had to adjust to attending high school in a place where all the Black kids throughout the district attended.

The school's name describes the historical perspective and impact the school had on the students and the Black community. The faculty was great and seriously concerned with preparing the students for life after graduation. Integration occurred during my tenth-grade year at Carver, so I started my junior year at Navasota High in 1969. I had just adjusted to being around all the Black kids within the district, so transferring to what was the "white school" was yet another life-altering experience for me.

I was taught that white folks looked upon Black people as inferior. I heard all the stories about the town and how Blacks were treated. I couldn't help but recall what Mama said:

"Stay in your place, and don't be looking at them white women."

We had no choice but to go to Navasota High, but I don't believe a single kid from Carver wanted to be there. A couple of the Black teachers from Carver transferred, so that helped because we had someone we related to. After settling in, I realized it really wasn't that bad because it appeared as though the teachers accepted their role as educators, and the students got along. When Black athletes started to make significant improvements within the athletic programs, the overall atmosphere on campus got better. I still remembered what Mama had said.

I successfully completed my junior and senior years and graduated with the class of 1970 from Navasota High School on May 23, 1970, and, boy, was I happy !

I proudly walked onto the stage to receive my high school diploma and walked off, glad to be finished with high school. I received my diploma but no guidance on furthering my education. I ranked among the top 50 of my graduating class but still had no idea about what I would face in the real world. It wouldn't have mattered because my parents didn't have the money to send me to college.

JT graduated with the class of 1969 and was already in Houston. He moved in with Sister and went to work in road construction where our daddy worked. Not very long after he moved to Houston, Uncle Sam sent him a letter. The Vietnam conflict was winding down, but young men were still needed. He was invited to report to the testing place in Bryan, Texas, and the next thing I knew, he was headed to Fort Polk in Louisiana for basic training and afterward to Fort Bennings in Georgia for airborne training. After completing his training, he was off to Vietnam.

For most of my senior year at Navasota High, JT was dodging bullets in another country. He would send a letter home now and again, and Mama would send him a care package when money allowed. Then, the news came that he had been wounded. I'm not sure just how Mama dealt with what had been reported, but I'm sure she was relieved to learn his wounds were not life-threatening and that he was getting treatment in a hospital in Okinawa. After JT recovered and his tour was completed, he didn't re-up. He again moved back with Sister and went to work for the City of Houston. To this day, he still won't talk much about his experience in Vietnam, but what he will share is not pretty.

After I graduated, I worked on the ranch just long enough to buy a Greyhound bus ticket to Houston. I headed to Sister's house with about $25 in my pocket. I had no idea what was next but was happy to be leaving. Sister lived with our daddy when she first went to Houston in the Fourth Ward section of the city until she married. The Fourth Ward was an area where most residents were predominantly Black. It was similar to back home in that everybody knew everyone and kept an eye out for one another. Many of the elder women in Fourth Ward kept the kids for working parents and helped with their raising. Many people rented houses owned by one man, Mr. Anthony, and the rent was affordable. By now, Sister had become a single parent, had a child she named Rechelle, and lived in a house on O'Neal Street. JT and I stayed with her for a while until he married and moved into his own place.

As she had done when we were kids, Sister provided that mama-like sense of security. She gave each of us a place to stay when we left home and never asked us to pay for anything. I believe, at some point, we all lived with Sister in the house on O'Neal Street. After leaving home, we were so occupied with life that some of our closeness disappeared. Although I know we never lost love for one another, we were just occupied with other things. I guess that was the way it was supposed to be.

``For years, we all did our own thing. JT was always a little hot-headed and displayed many of Daddy's traits. At one point, he wanted to be a Golden Gloves boxer—that was until he got popped in the eye! He took the gloves off and has been packing a knife ever since. He really wanted to be a police officer after getting out of service but was too light in the britches to qualify. I chased women like Daddy, and I had that country swag. Jr. was always self-conscience of his speech impediment but got sipping the sauce from Daddy, as well. Irene was fortunate enough to attend and graduate from Sam Houston State. After graduating, she married Mr. James Gamble and moved to San Antonio. She took after Mama in many ways. Connie, on the other hand, took on a lot of GG's traits. However, we all were instilled with the importance of working for what we got.

`I didn't venture out too far because things in Houston moved a little bit faster than I was used to. There were so many unfamiliar sounds like police and ambulance sirens, big, tall buildings, and so many pretty little things that I didn't know which to get after first. It didn't take long for me to get up to speed. You see, having that country swag helped. I figured I wouldn't have any problem because those city girls hadn't seen a "Country Casanova" before.

Honestly speaking, God and the church got lost in the fog back then.

Shortly after I arrived in Houston, I got a job stocking groceries at a corner store. Although this was not a real job, it provided a source of income, and I was able to help Sister with a bill or two. I saw working at the store as an opportunity to pitch my line because a lot of pretty little things came in. I threw my line out, and the catches weren't bad. I caught my share of throwbacks, but a few keepers were in the bunch. While working at the store, I watched the butcher cut meat, so I figured I could too. Believe it or not, I learned all the cuts of pork and beef and managed the meat counter when the butcher was out. By then, I felt I had become an asset to the owner, but he saw it differently and refused to pay additional wages. I soon left and got hired as a busboy at a restaurant. While working there, I had my first experience seeing marijuana. I thought it was alfalfa hay!

One of the guys who worked there had a matchbox filled with what looked like hay to me. During breaks, he would roll it up and smoke. Because it had an unfamiliar smell, I asked what it was. He said it was weed and offered me some. I burned out like a scaled dog going through a one-light town. This country boy wasn't with smoking hay!

I had gotten close to a pretty little thing in the hood, and things were going really good…so good until she said, "I'm pregnant." Many young men have heard those words before, so you know what my response was: "What you mean you pregnant?"

Mama always told me,

"Boy, if you fool around and 'big one' of them little girls, you better do the right thing."

I wasn't ready for the responsibility of taking care of a baby, but I refused to be like my daddy. I had no idea or plans on how to handle this new phase of my life, but there was no stopping what was coming. With the little money I was making at the time, there was no way I could take care of a family. Despite that, we got married. Many seem to think the reason things end up the way they do is because of their smarts. I believe it's divine intervention.

Not long after getting married with a baby on the way, JT told me the City of Houston was hiring. I interviewed for employment with the Street Repair Division and was hired on October 10, 1972. With a new job making more money, I thought big things would soon happen. I didn't realize it then, but God was just making a way for what was to come, and on January 1, 1973, our little bundle of joy made her entrance into the world. We named her Rochanda but called her Shon. Now I had the means to care for my family.

We rented a house in Fourth Ward and started life as a young family. I tried to learn all I could from the men with years of service on the job and watched and questioned the older guys about everything. I didn't remain a common laborer long because one particular old guy took me under his wing. He would say things to me like,

> *"Junior, you ain't like all them other young fellows here. You come to work every day. They call in sick every time they accumulate a few hours. They ain't sick. If you ain't sick, save your sick time; it's like money in the bank. If you have a real sickness, you can still draw a paycheck. The city will pay you for the sick and vacation time you got saved if you stay long enough to retire. Then, go and get a commercial driver's license and take the driver's test they post on the board."*

At that time, Black employees were finally allowed to supervise a work crew. I guess because they had to endure The Man's wrath and worked like a slave when whites held all supervisory positions, they worked the hell out of us when they got to be boss. Although hard work wasn't foreign to me, it was the downside of my new job. The upside was many of the new Black crew supervisors were limited in their reading and writing skills, so I volunteered to complete the work orders detailing that day's work for them. I looked at this as an opportunity to learn. You never know who is watching you. One will experience many ups and downs during life, and many tend to be within the employment field. The key to survival is looking at the good and bad and seeing opportunities to learn and grow.

Not long after I went to work for the city, our daddy passed. Even though we lived in the same area, I never really had a relationship with him. Now, don't get this twisted—I respected the fact that he was my dad and was still due respect as an adult. In my opinion, I extended to him the respect he deserved. Life was short-lived for him, as he was only 49 years of age at the time of his death. A history of smoking, drinking, and life in the fast lane may have contributed to an early demise. I found it difficult to grieve his passing, for I knew him only as the person who sired me, but I did not consider him a father. At his funeral, I noticed Mama crying. Mind you, he was the person who never did right by his responsibilities regarding her and his kids, so after the service, I asked Mama why she cried. She reminded me that even though they had been long since divorced and she was happy, he was still our daddy, so if one of us hurt, she did too. I'm sure Mama endured many occasions of feeling deserted and worried about what our next meal would look like, but this was one of the few times I saw my Mama cry.

Not long after my daddy's passing, trouble began in my home. Now, I probably contributed to some of the humbugs because even though I had been married for a while with a kid, I, unfortunately, had my daddy's genes and still wanted to chase the pretty little things. I thought I could balance the two but always told myself I never wanted to be like Daddy. With both my wife and I being young and living in and around relatives, the influence of those lifestyles affected how we got along. When I first saw that little hot mama, I had one thing in mind and didn't consider family history; I was looking for a good time. Just as I had my daddy's genes, she apparently had her share of her family genes. No one gets to choose who their parents are, but we do have a choice in how our life turns out. At the time, she wasn't ready to be tied down with a family to raise. The nightlife seemed more to her liking. I am not throwing shade or placing blame, for I also take accountability for my role in a failed marriage. Although a beautiful baby girl was a product of this union, I'd advise anyone to examine the entire family's history before taking on a mate.

History serves to remind us of what occurred in the past and provides a vision of the future. Having that knowledge, you shouldn't follow or behave like other family members. You decide your destiny. Because we were both easily influenced by others and what happened around us, our marriage went downhill quickly, and she left.

Regretting our marriage didn't last long, and her leaving took away my opportunity to be a father to my little girl. I was depressed. I wasn't able to keep my family together or have a hand in raising my child, and that hurt. I spent many nights in bed wishing for them, but the divorce decree outlined who got what and how visitations were to be. Mama didn't say much, but I'm sure she thought I would turn out just like my daddy. After a period of depression and thinking about what I could do to right my wrong, I finally arrived at the conclusion that we were not meant to be. Because I was not built for looking back, I started to bait my lines again. Truth be told, I never really took my lines out of the water.

I was doing well at work and began to advance. I had a little more money and could buy a new outfit for the weekend scene, so dating wasn't a problem. By then, Sister had moved to another house, so I set up my bachelor pad in the house on O'Neal Street. My rascal buddy and I would try and one-up the other by having a different lady friend every Friday night at the house parties. All throughout the late 1970s, we spent almost every weekend twisting on the dance floor. There were ladies we just wanted to be seen with, but there were a few who made you feel different inside and provided some pleasant memories. I liked them all but, regretfully, can't remember all their names. Living the single life had its perks. I had a good job, rode around in a nice car, and had pretty little things going and coming. I thought I was set and didn't need much else.

Would you believe I went to Sam Houston State? Not for the reason of higher education. I went pretending to visit Irene, who was actually enrolled there. She was fortunate to attend college utilizing Daddy's Social Security benefits. Irene had a roommate and a lot of other girlfriends who liked to party. She also partook in her share of college life, so I saw this as an opportunity. This, for me, was like putting the opossum in the chicken coop. It didn't matter because none of the college girls wanted to hear my lies, so I stopped going to Sam Houston. I had enough back in Houston to keep me busy, so I didn't stress about not hooking up there. Now, I'll admit that having more than one line in the water can cause a problem or two, but nothing was too tough for me. It was all gas, no brakes.

After arriving in Houston, JT and I joined an amateur baseball team called the Houston Trailblazers. We both had developed a love of baseball while playing on little and pony league teams. We would play for several years with the Trailblazers until family life occupied his time, causing him to quit baseball. By now, Jr. had graduated and found his way to Houston. He also went to live with Sister. After he settled and found employment, he and I would play on the same teams. We would play on Sundays, so going to church was out of the question. Honestly speaking, I forgot about God and church. My only thoughts were where the next game would be and which pretty little thing would be with me. I thought I was a pretty good baseball player, and everywhere the team played, I had a PLT with me. I was like Jeter when it came to PLTs: I caught everything, bobbled a few, and after the game was over, got ready for the next.

One particular game I vividly remember because our team had traveled to San Antonio to play a team that had dominated us every time we played. At the game, I twisted my ankle sliding into second base, and my PLT almost made it out to the base before any of my teammates. After a few minutes, I was able to walk it off and finish the game. This would be the only time we defeated the dominating team, and guess who was on the pitcher's mound. You guessed it! Me, the little left-handed pitcher with a wicked curve ball. Having my sweetie make a fuss over me and my injury was the icing on the cake.

Later, Jr. and I would join the Houston Black Sox. This team was organized by several guys we knew from the country and played games in the Men's Senior Baseball Association.

Most games were scheduled in and around Houston and the Bryan College Station area. At the end of the regular season, qualifying teams would be invited to travel to Phoenix, Arizona, to play in a week-long tournament of games in what the organization called their World Series. Baseball teams from across the U.S., Canada, and Mexico were all represented. Our team secured trips to Phoenix in 1993, 1994, and 1995 from regular season wins.

For the love of the game, each player paid all expenses out-of-pocket. This was nothing like the major leagues because if you didn't have the money to pay, you didn't play. Overall, what an experience it was to play on the same baseball diamonds major league baseball teams used during spring training!

Our teams were pretty good but never got to the championship game, and after playing for over 20 years, I lost the itch to play baseball around 1999 and retired my bat and ball. I still loved the game and thought about playing, but since I couldn't rooster like I used to, I thought I had better stay out of the chicken coop!

Playing baseball provided an opportunity for me to do something I loved and took my mind off real-world stuff. You see, baseball is just a game, but you will have to face and deal with the real world at some point.

Chapter Five

A Lady's Influence

To fill in some important years, I'll need to go back to the mid-1970s when something happened that would forever impact my life. One morning, I was driving to work when I noticed three girls at a bus stop. All were waiting for the school bus and, I guess, thinking of that day's activities. They could have been talking about boys—I don't know. I know what I had in mind. One girl was particularly tuff, and the pants she had on fit her backside just right. You know, her backfield was in motion. She was also easy on the eyes. I thought to myself how I wanted that one and stopped to get her digits. I figured I would find the right lie to tell and show her off at the next house party, but the girl was much sharper than I thought and already had me pegged. She ended up giving me a bad telephone number and told me her name was Carolyn. After failing to contact her, I chalked it up as just another one that had gotten away.

Anyway, I was already involved in a relationship with a nice lady, and we were always together. We had been dating for a good while, so I didn't stress about missing Carolyn. Who knows? If I hadn't been such a rascal and done right by the lady I dated, there might have been a future for us. That was until I ran across Carolyn again while slow-rolling through Third Ward. I approached her again with my country swag and called her hand about giving me bad information. This time, she provided her real name, Ernestine, and telephone number. Hello! It was on then.

It must have been something I said that day, for we hit it off this time and started to date on a serious level. Although things were going well, I put the lady I had been dating on the back burner and moved Ernestine to the front. Remember, she was the PLT who fussed over me when I sprained my ankle. I figured this wouldn't take long because I was sure I could easily fool this youngster. I simply wanted to stick and move, then move on to my next victim so I could keep my Player's Card in good standing. It wasn't long before I found out she was far from being a dumb bunny. Having realized this might take longer than expected, I still kept my old friend on a slow simmer just in case.

Ernestine became the PLT seen with me at the house parties and baseball games. I thought a movie now and again, dinner a time or two, appearances at house parties, and Sunday games would keep her satisfied. By now, I was letting her drive my new 1979 Z28 Camaro I purchased from a local dealership's showroom. Who wouldn't be satisfied riding through the hood in a fast car? Well, after dating a few years, she came by one afternoon with an ultimatum. She said that day would be the day I decided what we were going to do. We were either going to get married or, after she left, it was over. To put it frankly, she said I had to shit or get off the pot. Ernestine had tolerated my misbehaving; she had accepted my daughter Shon and, throughout our courtship, took her everywhere she went when it was my weekend to have her.

As I mentioned before, she was smart beyond her years and wanted more than just to have a good time. Being faced with her ultimatum was another life-changing moment. I had already experienced marriage, and it didn't go well. I had a good job, a new car, my own crib, and a steady girlfriend, and I still hooked up with side pieces every now and again. What else is there?

I had managed to keep things afloat so far. Or so I thought. I would always tell Ernestine we would get married when this happened or that happened. Furthermore, the others were just friends, but she didn't believe my lies and wanted a firm commitment. She was done listening to my lies. Well, I didn't want the fellas teasing me about what happened to that lady who was always with me, so I had to seriously consider my next move.

It's now the bottom of the ninth with two outs and two strikes on me. I had one swing left, but the one thing I didn't have was time. I knew Ernestine meant what she said. What the hell? I didn't want to lose her and have the fellas tease me, and I certainly didn't want to see her with someone else. So, I did what needed to be done. After five years of dating, down the aisle we went.

I didn't realize it then, but that day in October 1981, after becoming Nelson and Ernestine J. Marsh, I had united with my lifelong partner.

I spent many years chasing women just for pleasure and a baseball, hoping to win a championship ring. It would take a few years to realize I had found something better when she put a gold band on my left hand. I had hooked a keeper this time, and Mama liked her too. Being married isn't bad if both parties are committed to what the preacher tells them to repeat. Even though I repeated everything the preacher said, I still liked PLTs. Needless to say, some habits are hard to let go. She committed to her role in the marriage and loved helping with Shon when she spent weekends with us. I, on the other hand, still thought I was a player.

After we had been married for about four years, Ernestine came home one afternoon crying and said, "I'm pregnant!" That little booger made his appearance on July 4, 1985, and we named him Nelson Dwayne. I initially thought the nurse had brought the wrong baby to the waiting room because, to me, he looked like E.T.

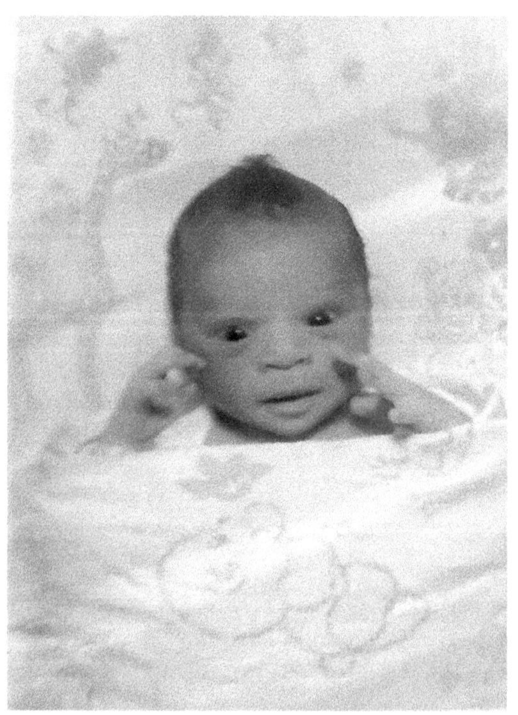

After he was born, no more sports cars for Ernestine. She had to drive a "Mommy Mobile." Four years later, she again came to me crying and uttered the words, "I'm pregnant." Man, how did that happen? Only this time, the nurse came to the waiting room with a beautiful baby girl

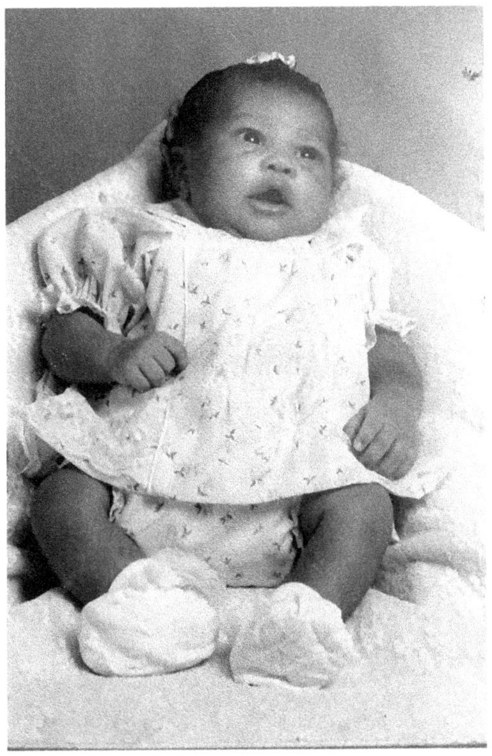

She arrived on September 8, 1989, and we named her Tiffany Lashay. We were now a family of four with a boy and a girl, and, at this point, we needed a station wagon! Really, we were five because Ernestine accepted Shon as her own and had a hand in helping raise her.

Ernestine worked in retail, and it required her to be away evenings. Back then, I practically raised the kids on burgers and chicken nuggets from Dairy Queen. Having kids is pleasant when they are little because they can be so lovable. Man, does that change as they grow up! You wish you could send them back to wherever. You would probably commit murder if you thought you could get away with it. Maybe not. It never crossed my mind, and I loved being a father. Both kids began their pre-schooling, attending Advent Presbyterian Academy and grade school at Bethel Christian Academy. After school, the Stay and Play Daycare facility would pick them up, and I would get them after work.

The kids started to develop their identity early. Because I loved the game of baseball, we started Nelson Dwayne in Little League baseball. He did okay for a while but started to linger in schoolwork, and as he grew older, he was intrigued by things other kids were doing. We decided that baseball was not a good choice. On the other hand, Tiffany always had a mind of her own. All while she was in daycare, pre-k, and Kindergarten, Ernestine would dress and comb her hair in the mornings. If mom was working, I would comb her hair as Ernestine did. I thought I did as good of a job as her mom, but her hairstyle was never the same when I would pick them up after school. I don't know how or when, but it was never as I combed it.

Chapter Six

Several Trying Years

As a family, we would travel home to spend most of the holidays with Mama Lois and GG. You could expect everybody to be home for Easter weekend and Christmas. We would attend church together, exchange a gift or two, and enjoy Mama's cooking. The house would be filled with good cheer and the aroma of home-cooked food. Having family members all together was always a memorable time.

GG always owned a few heads of cattle but never owned property to keep them on. He would rent property, but the locations never had good fencing. Jr., little Nelson, and I spent many weekends repairing fences. That changed in 1989 when GG got hurt wrangling cattle on his job. It was a traumatic accident whereby his leg was broken, and he had a stroke by the time he received medical help. He never really adjusted to his disabilities and refused to do rehab, so Mama took the brunt of his frustrations. Even though he could not work, he still wanted to own cattle, so I went to the country on weekends.

For all that Mama had gone through raising us alone until GG came, there was nothing I wouldn't do whether she asked or not. Again, Mama never let us know how mean GG had become and didn't let it be known how difficult of a time she was having.

In the meantime, I took the old employee's advice and started to move up in the ranks. I began as a laborer and was promoted to truck driver, equipment operator, and assistant supervisor. To put this into perspective, at that time, I was around 28 years old, Black, and in an organization that was top-heavy with whites. I took advantage of all the opportunities the company afforded me, but I will admit it was during a time when a certain number of minorities had to be included. I did everything that was required of an assistant and took on most of the tasks the supervisor should have completed. You already know how this works: the white supervisor sat back and waited until I completed the morning activities like checking attendance, scheduling the work crews, and placing the documents on his desk. He would sign off on whatever I placed on his desk, and off he went. The responsibility for following up and verifying the work fell upon me. I'm not sure what he spent his day doing, but who was I to question it? I'm sure you can relate to doing the work they proudly take credit for. Nonetheless, I was preparing for something greater to come later. One may not realize it, but remember, someone is always watching.

A lot has transpired from my first settling in Houston to now. Again, I will admit I took for granted that God was always there, and I was a recipient of his grace. The things I did and some places I found myself would have turned out differently had He not watched over me. Also, because Mama was a praying woman, I know I'm the recipient of some of her prayers. Ernestine was also a church-going lady, so I'm sure she mentioned me in a few prayers. She and the kids would go to church on Sundays while that booger Nelson was off to who knows where or what. I'm not telling, but there's one other who does know.

The kids were doing okay. And Ernestine enjoyed being a mom, liked her job, and didn't give me much grief. I worked, played baseball, did other things, and the bills were being met. That was good enough for me, but had it not been for her tolerance of my misdoings, we wouldn't be where we are today. Even with me still moving and shaking, being home at night was important, although I might have missed one or two. That changed after I came in one morning to find Ernestine sitting in bed crying crocodile tears. I could tell she had been up all night. Lucky for me, she is not a violent person, but that look she had and what she said,

"Nelson, I'm not going looking for you or want to know what you were doing or who you were with. You should have the decency to call so I won't be worried, thinking something bad happened. That ain't right."

I knew then I wouldn't do that again. If I hadn't hidden the pistol, I might have been trying to dodge a bullet or some hot grits. I thought I could roll with whatever, but she meant her vows and was willing to trust God and wait for me to realize what I had.

One afternoon, as I came home from work, Ernestine met me at the door with a look that instantly made me wonder what she heard now. The worst news one could ever receive greeted me that afternoon in October 1991. She told me that Mama Lois had been rushed to a hospital in Bryan, Texas, and we needed to leave. When I asked what was wrong, she simply said we needed to go. If you asked me today where the kids were, I wouldn't be able to tell you. What I will say no one had to tell me. I knew at that moment that I would never see Mama alive again.

Ernestine drove because I didn't think it would have been safe if I got behind the wheel. When we arrived at the hospital, several of my siblings were already gathered outside, and the look on their faces confirmed my thoughts. As I approached, I asked, "Is Mama gone?" I'm unsure who answered, but I recall hearing, "She's dead!" Anyone who ever heard these words understands the hurt one feels to learn that the angel who carried you until birth, loved, nurtured, and instilled the values you carry will no longer be where she once was.

I heard what they said, but I had to see for myself. Having done so, I saw the appearance of "at peace" on Mama's face. After gathering ourselves, we realized that Mama had endured a lot while raising us as a single parent and after GG got hurt when he became mean and abusive. God saw fit to call her home, but not before he granted her wish to see her kids become adults.

Mama left us some thirty years ago, but I still find comfort in visiting her gravesite just to talk. After she passed, going home just didn't feel like home anymore, so gathering as a family ceased. GG did okay alone, coping with his disabilities but failed to pay property taxes for several years, and foreclosure proceedings were initiated on the property he and Mama owned. While Mama was living, they often had heated discussions about the matter, but it appears he made partial or no payment. By now, there was a significant amount due to avoid losing the property, so my siblings and I gathered to discuss how we would handle the matter. We knew GG had no means to satisfy the taxes at the time but needed a place to stay where he was comfortable, so the taxes had to be paid.

Due to their own financial commitments, it was difficult for my siblings to take on an added expense. After discussing the matter with Mrs. Marsh, we decided to satisfy the delinquent taxes. I had a lengthy discussion with GG about the matter, and he agreed to make yearly payments towards the amount owed as he sold his calf crop. I still felt a lean on the property was necessary as collateral and security for our investment. He knew that if the taxes were not paid, he would lose the property, and, secondly, I couldn't invest that amount of money without something as collateral. Having agreed to what was proposed, the agreement was notarized. If he satisfied the terms of the agreement, I would relinquish any interest I had.

Shortly after we paid the taxes, GG began to tell anyone who would listen I was trying to take his property. I admit I was blindsided and deeply hurt to learn he would do such a thing because I never saw him as being that type of person. Now I was being portrayed as a villain in the eyes of many, but they weren't knowledgeable of the entire story. I always looked at him as a great father figure; he had taught and done much for us. In that light, I never spoke with him about why he did such a thing, but you never really know a person until you REALLY know that person.

After a few years, he arranged to repay what I had invested through a law firm, and after doing so, I relinquished the interest I had in the property. Although settled, I had a different view of the man who once taught me so much.

Chapter Seven

Life as a Father and Public Servant

By 1996, my eldest daughter, Shon, had grown into a young lady. So much so that she said she was getting married. "What!!" Like any father, there's no joker good enough for your baby, and here's my daughter telling me she was about to marry some booger bear I didn't know anything about. Be that as it may, I wouldn't stand in her way if she wanted to marry that joker. I initially had doubts about him, but I guess she knew what she was doing all along because they have been happily married for well over 20 years and gave us our first grandbaby, Keana. I call her Big Thunder.

The City of Houston afforded me many opportunities, and I traveled to many places representing the city. Those opportunities exposed me to and enhanced my knowledge of how other cities operated. Being the rascal I was, I quickly realized those in decision-making positions were looked upon by some employees favorably. I quickly progressed from an entry-level to a supervisory role. After being promoted to supervisor, I became responsible for a complete section. Other opportunities were availed as I was asked to perform duties outside my classification. As part of my list of duties, I handled personnel matters from grievances to disciplinary concerns. I never complained and, instead, considered this as an opportunity to grow. After all, I was amongst plenty…you know!

I must have done well because I was considered for promotion to the position of section chief. I was responsible for personnel matters and managing the supervisors in charge of field operations. By this time, I had worked under many supervisors on my way to this position. Now, they would report to me!

Dressing in nice business suits, traveling as a city representative, and occupying an office in the main building, I figured I should take advantage of all the perks my position afforded. With this new position and without wading in too deep, let's just say some things should remain private, and furthermore, I'm not one to kiss and tell.

Picture it: a Black man occupying an office in the administration building, younger than many of the employees he now managed. Things were going well. A few years earlier, the city started to hire female employees in its field operations section. There was no stopping me. I took the brakes out and pressed hard on the accelerator. I knew better; I was just too young to care!

Once promoted, I'm sure many fostered ill intentions and thoughts that I would be vindictive and remember what they had done, but my message was clear. I was intent on doing my job, so if they did theirs, we didn't have a problem. If not, I wouldn't risk losing my job because someone didn't do theirs. Luckily, things never got too stressful because I worked to earn their respect, and they respected my authority. Remember I told you that we're always being watched and tested. Well, another test came one day as the division manager came to my office and invited me to lunch. He ordered what he wanted for lunch and a cocktail and invited me to do the same. Consuming alcohol while at work violated policy, so I got a burger and a Coke. I didn't drink alcohol, however; if I did, it wouldn't have happened with the boss.

After a few years of occupying the position of section chief, the manager was accused of misappropriating funds and soon resigned. After a complete restructuring of the division, I was promoted to general maintenance manager. I was now responsible for maintaining all city rights of way and still didn't drink. The only downside of being in this position was I had to attend various civic club meetings and answer angry citizens' questions.

This promotion also meant getting home late some nights after being shouted at by citizens, but the opportunities the position offered made it all worthwhile. Not to sound repetitive, but you're always being watched. As I attended a National Hurricane Conference in Orlando, Florida, a well-known weather reporter from Houston approached me with a microphone in a hallway during a seminar break. I had no idea a weather reporter from Houston was there, but he knew I was. I wasn't prepared to be interviewed, but my comments were aired as recorded during his evening weather broadcast. A few years later, I applied and was promoted to deputy assistant director with the responsibilities for managing a $30,000,000 budget, 430 full-time positions (many of whom I worked alongside through the ranks), salaries, performances, disciplinary matters, and equipment needs. Five out of the total employee count reported to me.

Chapter Eight

A Test of Resilience

By now, we had outgrown the apartment we called home for several years and needed a larger place to live. We found a house to lease and moved in. The kids, who had been attending private school, would now attend public school. We weren't that concerned because they had been provided with a firm foundation, and we did well as parents. Having spent several years at Bethel Christian Academy and sheltered from real-world stuff, we felt confident that what we had taught and shown them would offset the influences they'd face in a public school. Around this time, Ernestine decided to leave the retail field and enter the healthcare profession. We dealt with the normal issues all parents with school-age kids go through daily, and our next few years were rather normal. At this stage, kids start needing deodorant, their hormones kick in, and parents start catching hell. They begin to think they can do what they see their friend do. They soon realized it wasn't happening in our house.

Things got interesting at work after an investigation conducted by a local news reporter suggested that the maintenance division had inflated the number of potholes that were being repaired. I wasn't too stressed about the investigation because the reporting process had been constant for years and could be explained. However, following the election of a new mayor, the reporting process made for a hot story and appeared on the five o'clock news broadcasts. I knew my interview with the reporter would be edited and not aired as recorded. Naturally, if you pay attention to any news story, they are often slanted and edited to suggest wrongdoings. One of the newly elected mayor's campaign promises was to fix the pothole problem. The news report suggested that the numbers were overly reported to support that promise. The person I reported to didn't wish to own any part of the responsibility in addressing a controversial situation because he was appointed by the new administration. I soon realized I could become the fall guy simply by being the only person of color who occupied a position of responsibility. By now, I had the required years of service and age to exceed the requirements of receiving full retirement, so I submitted my application.

Now, I know how my people think, and the truth is never juicy enough. They would rather hear, "they ran him off." Sadly, it's normally your own people who wish to see you fail. We'll believe a lie anytime over the truth, and each time the lie gets told, we put our own spin on it. The truth is that my application was received and approved after spending 29 years with the company. I retired with full benefits on June 1, 2001, at 48 years old.

Remember, I was hired as a laborer, and to retire two levels below the director of public works is something that could not have happened without my determination to be the best I could be and God's blessing. One may be able to reach lofty goals, but if God has not blessed their path, I believe it's short-lived and not as satisfying. Looking back at my accomplishments, I think I did well. I never wished to be given anything and worked to earn all I received and left with the satisfaction of knowing that many opportunities for others were made available regarding employment and advancement during my time in management with the City of Houston. Others might perceive this as boasting, but my progression speaks for itself.

Shortly after retiring, breaking news reported a plane had crashed into the World Trade Center. Many can recall where they were and what they were doing when it occurred, and like millions of other people, I stared at the television screen, trying to make sense of what was happening. America was under attack! I couldn't believe what was happening to the most powerful nation on earth. Just like Kennedy's assassination in 1963, the tragedy of September 11, 2001, was witnessed by millions as it was shown in real time.

To see people take the leap of death is probably the worst thing I have ever seen. It also reminded me that you never know where your last moments will find you. The visuals of the towers falling will forever remain etched in my memory and further remind me I won't have time to get it right. Instead, I need to keep it right with my heavenly father because His will shall be done. Many lives were lost that day, and a void forever left in the hearts of family members. It took America ten years to achieve its commitment to track down the mastermind and hold them accountable for what happened.

Following the tragedy of September 11th and all that took place thereafter, I thought I could settle into enjoying retirement. But just when you think everything is going well, all hell breaks loose!

We received notice in early July 2002 that the lease agreement on the house would not be renewed. Unknown to us, the property had been sold, and we had to move. Purchasing a house wasn't a thought at the time, but I knew moving into another apartment wouldn't be an option. I needed a place for my family and quick! I had no idea where to start, but I knew I wasn't alone and believed God had planned things this way. With His guidance, I found and closed on a new home for my family in less than 60 days. God can fix anything!

After we moved in October 2002, I spent the next few years transporting the kids to and from school. Each day, as we'd commute, I would discuss real-life issues and remind them that all decisions have consequences. I'd emphasize that every decision they make has a result attached, and they must be responsible and own the results. Not long after settling into our new home, Ernestine began to excel in her new career, and, as before, on Sundays, she and the kids would attend church. On the other hand, I was still moving around and thought there wouldn't be a problem because I never neglected my responsibilities at home. What I didn't initially realize is that there's more to being a husband and father than just making sure the bills are paid.

Chapter Nine

Kids Are Challenging

Our son, Nelson Dwayne, graduated from Eisenhower High School in 2003 and was accepted at Prairie View A&M University. However, after one semester, he didn't have the grades to continue because he was unprepared for college courses and didn't adjust well. The things he experienced on "The Hill" didn't help. The rules imposed while at home no longer applied, and he viewed college life as the opportunity to experience the things he previously couldn't. And, boy, did he hit the gas! All gas and no brakes are an understatement. I wonder where he got that from…

If you recall, he was born July 4th, so one might expect fireworks to go off. I was disappointed because we had discussed so much while commuting to high school. Knowing life's challenges, we didn't give up and enrolled him in a local two-year college. Being home, he did well and, after a year improved his GPA enough to be accepted back on campus at Prairie View, and again, we allowed him to return to The Hill. Unfortunately, he still struggled, engaged in previous activities, and again became academically suspended. As parents, we try our hardest and want our kids to be successful, but I'm sure today he regrets missing an opportunity many wish for. It's still early, but the right lady will change a man. I believe Nelson Dwayne found that lady, and he is no longer all gas and no brakes. He's now married to Mrs. Nikki Marsh and raising their kids, Al-Eyah, Fariah, and Kaysen.

Our daughter, Tiffany, graduated from Eisenhower High School in 2007 and chose Lamar University to continue her education. She elected to study criminal justice for three years before deciding to transfer to Texas Southern University. She explained the transfer by saying it would be easier for her to be accepted into their law program—if she had actually registered for school. For whatever reason, she left college before completing her last year and gave no explanation as to why.

As young adults, both made some bad decisions regarding their continued education and life in general. Naturally, as parents, we have dreams about our kid's future, but most of the time, it's never what you wish for. They end up doing it their way. Only after the train derails do they seek your counsel. Fussing and using choice words won't help resolve anything. We were once there, so we know the results of dumb decisions. Even so, it's hard to resist saying, "You knew better. I told you what could happen." Rehashing what's already happened changes nothing. Instead, your time is better spent by remaining an adult and, together, figuring out how to move forward while minimizing the chance of repeating the same mistakes. Sometimes, the lessons they learn from bumping their head can have more value than a return on the money you invested. Life can teach some things that college courses simply cannot. Then again, college isn't for everyone.

Both Nelson Dwayne and Tiffany stumbled their way through some trying times. However, they have since made course corrections and are doing better. Mama often said,

"When you have done your best, give it to God."

Although I worried constantly about both kids during their difficult years, I had to pray, wait, and watch. I know you can't rush God, but it can certainly get tough during the wait. After your kids are old enough to be considered young adults, parents must rely on what they instilled and trust their faith in God. I'm sure the idea of disappointing a parent and embarrassment is a heavy weight to bear. I know I never wanted to face Mama after it came to light that I did the very thing she told me not to do. With all my fussing and cussing, we never stopped supporting them. Ernestine would only say, "I just can't turn my back. They are still my children."

Tiffany's job relocated her to the Dallas area following the devastation caused by Hurricane Harvey. This caused her to be away from a comfortable environment, which was a blessing. She was forced out of her comfort zone and had to face the real world alone. I often shared with her that I left home with nothing but a determination to make it. I advised her to formulate her own identity and assert herself with confidence. One should never be afraid to engage in conversation with anyone, but always be sure of your words. Respect the other person's opinion, but if it contradicts your values, don't be afraid to tell them you disagree. Those who really know her will tell you she's a strong, determined, confident woman who has set some lofty goals. She found a new church home in the Dallas area and is actively involved there. She still loves to sing and is beginning to spread her wings as she pursues her passion for music. She's still single but has two dogs who think they are human.

Our oldest daughter, Shon, her husband Desmond, and Keana 'Big Thunder' are doing well. Even though I could only be there for short visits during Shon's younger years, we cherish the joy they bring to our lives. Although she's the oldest, she's still a daddy's baby. I am grateful for the time she spent with us as a child and proud of the lady she became. Knowing that our kids were introduced to God's word early gives me a sense of comfort that they will be okay. I found the writings in the book of Proverbs to be easily understood, and the book speaks to just about everything one will face in life.

Chapter Ten

Events Which Impacted My Life

Another history-making event I thought I would never see happened in 2008. I witnessed the election of a Black American President. I am probably amongst the many who had similar thoughts considering the methods of modern-day slavery. Still, America witnessed the election and swearing-in of Barack Obama as the 44th President of the United States of America. I'd be willing to bet that most Black Baby Boomers, Generation X, Millennials, and Generation Z have no idea what this meant. To have a Black man elected to the presidency of this nation is certainly a testament that anything is possible if you put in the work. If you don't know what your ancestors endured to make it possible for you to reach this point, you can't appreciate where you are. The knowledge regarding the history of Blacks in America should ignite something within. If not, we have a problem. We must never settle for "just okay." We must believe that we can then put in the work. Motivate yourself, and don't let anyone determine your legacy.

I thought after retiring, I would have time to finish my "do-nothing" list. During my tenure with the city, I became acquainted with an older gentleman, Mr. Henry, who enjoyed the outdoors. Hunting was always something I enjoyed doing, so he and I talked about it often. We became good friends and went on a few hunting trips together. After he retired, he and his wife needed some repairs done at their house. With me having little to do, I offered my help. I had some knowledge of the needed repairs, so I offered to do the work pro bono if they agreed. They allowed me to do the work; they only had to pay for materials. When the work was completed, they were happy and had saved some money. I've always enjoyed the company of older folks because one can learn so much from those who have experienced life and are full of wisdom. I would often visit just to talk, but more so, his wife could cook some good groceries! While we worked on the house, she would prepare lunch for us. She knew her way around the kitchen and could rustle up some pretty good grub. Her cooking reminded me of Mama's.

In early 2004, I received a phone call from the Henrys asking if I could come over. I didn't have a clue as to what they wanted, but I learned they had spoken with Mrs. Henry's niece regarding their last will and testament. Neither he nor his wife had children, so they were considering her as the beneficiary of their estate upon their demise. They managed their affairs but lived on a fixed income as most senior citizens. After speaking with her niece, they indicated that she didn't want "this old house" and posed the question, "What can we do with this old house?" Frankly, they owned a small single-family wood frame house built early in the 40s but was well maintained. The exchange made them feel disrespected because they had thought of her. To have her respond in that manner pissed them off! Not wanting the state to take over the estate, they decided to name me their beneficiary. I was humbled that they had considered me, yet I told them I thought it would be better if they considered someone else. Nothing I said changed their mind. I was firmly advised that I couldn't tell them what to do with their stuff! I would visit often to talk with them about many things. Both had experienced much and gained wisdom about many subjects, so I tried to extract from them that knowledge. My relationship with them grew so much that they began to call me Little Boy.

I would receive another call in late April 2005 from the wife asking me to come by. The husband had been dealing with several health concerns and wasn't feeling well. When I arrived, it was apparent that he was very ill, but he refused her request to go to the doctor. With some strong encouragement, we convinced him to go to the emergency room. After being hospitalized, he realized he might not get well enough to return home, so Mr. Henry asked me to promise him that I would see after his wife if he didn't make it back home. He appeared at peace and stated, "I'm all right. Don't worry about me." Wow! To have someone request such a promise from you will test anyone's metal. Mama often reminded us of God's commandment to treat others as you would want to be treated. You never know what tomorrow might hold for you or who might need to help you along the way. So, without hesitating, I told him I would do as he requested.

As I prepared to leave the hospital, his wife and I spoke briefly with the doctors. They didn't have promising news, for he was truly ill. I wanted to stay with her, but she insisted I go home to check on my family. The next day, April 23, 2005, I got the phone call. Since that day, the "Little Boy" remained committed to his promise to Mr. Henry. I didn't understand it then, but now I realize God had a plan for everything, and I was meant to be included. Having spent so much time with her since his passing, I gained a greater fondness for her. I gave her a nickname, too. I call her Hazel.

Hazel also dealt with health issues, but for the most part, she did okay. Prescription meds managed her health issues, but during one doctor's visit in 2007, she was advised that she would need to undergo a mastectomy because her lab results detected a concern. She handled this as she had everything else: she accepted the news and, without hesitating, decided to schedule the procedure. After the surgery, as I visited her in recovery, she joked that the doctor had taken her titty! Following all the therapies associated with breast cancer, doctors declared her cancer-free five years later.

Later, in 2011, we endured another health concern as she suffered a stroke that affected her speech and caused minor mobility concerns. After she was discharged from the hospital, we completed weekly speech therapy sessions and physical rehab at TIERR in the Medical Center for about a year. The therapy improved her speech to where she can hold a conversation without much difficulty, and her mobility can be surprising for someone her age and medical history. Her memory was never affected, as her ability to recall is amazing. Having gone through so much, she remains independent and performs most daily chores without difficulties. I now make daily visits just to check on her. I didn't think it would be safe for her to cook with her medical conditions, so we provide her with the foods she likes. It has been many years since I gave my word that day in 2005, and I have no regrets.

If that wasn't enough, having committed to be there for Hazel, Ernestine took sick in April 2012 and was hospitalized. When you witness the pain a loved one endures as they deal with sickness, you wonder if there is something you can do to lessen their pain. If I could have taken her place, I would have. I felt helpless but not hopeless because I remembered what Mama said. I often thought I would have to live without the person I loved so dearly, but reminded myself that when you have done all you can, you give it to God. I simply asked God to allow us the strength and understanding to make it through the challenges we faced. After spending a week hospitalized and following many doctors' visits for almost two years, we began the road to recovery. Thankfully, she's doing well today. Strangely enough, the doctors never explained what caused her illness in terms we understood. Although they have the training and skills to be doctors, there are some things only God can fix. When Ernestine was well enough to attend church again, I made a commitment to accompany her as a husband should. Now, I look forward to Sunday mornings, but the devil is always busy. I find myself getting upset because she takes forever to get dressed. I'm a stickler for being on time, but I think she likes getting under my skin.

Going through such a period will make a fella rearrange his priorities and conclude its time out for foolishness. But sometimes, God uses tough love to get our attention. I knew then it was time out for the "all gas and no brakes" way of living. Before, I took so much for granted. I kept saying I would make up my mind to return to church, but I wasn't ready and had some things I needed to get right before committing. Church was the place I needed to be in order to hear what I needed. It had been a long time since the mourning bench, my baptism, and regularly attending church services. God's mercy and the grace extended to Ernestine was what it took for me. I didn't deserve it, but what a blessing! And I'm thankful.

Chapter Eleven

Years Filled with Good, Bad, and Better Times

Today, families are faced with the challenges of present-day society; they no longer come together to reconnect with relatives. Church homecomings or family reunions used to be commonplace. Families gathered to visit those they had not seen during the year, partake in a good home-cooked meal, and introduce any new members to the family. We no longer know who and where our relatives are and go years without connecting with one another.

Remembering how we used to gather, I decided to organize a family reunion where we would meet and spend a day reconnecting and getting acquainted. Our first gathering in 2014 was well attended, and those who came expressed their appreciation for the opportunity to see many relatives they had not seen for years. Many also expressed a desire to see the reunion continue. During 2015 and 2016, we gathered in great numbers, but negative attitudes behind the scenes overshadowed the positive, so I decided not to be involved as the organizer in 2017's efforts. In everything, one must acknowledge the truth—the good and the bad—because one's growth depends on realizing which role one plays. I thought if I was not involved, some other family member would see the importance of carrying it forward. But sadly, no one decided to undertake the responsibility as the organizer, so we no longer gather as a family.

Much of what our elders felt was important to the family structure has been forgotten. Naturally, there will always be sibling rivalry in every family, but I never dreamed it could get to the point of envy. I didn't realize that kind of animosity was amongst us, but time will reveal everything. I regret we did not work out our differences and see the importance of taking the time to fellowship with one another. Scripture, as recorded in Psalms 133, teaches about fellowshipping together. One can always say, "I'll do it when I get the time," …until you can't. Tomorrow may not come.

I realize I continue to say, "You are always being watched," but you are. As Ernestine recovered from her illness, she noticed me watching the Kentucky Derby on television. Earlier, I reported that we had a difficult couple of years, not knowing what was happening or what our future would look like. After recovering well enough to be permitted by her doctors to return to work, she came home one afternoon and surprised me, saying, "Honey, we're going to the Derby!" What! Me, going to the Derby? Well, we did and sat along the first turn at Churchill Downs when the horse, named American Pharoah, won the 2015 Run for the Roses.

I even got the pictures and souvenirs to prove it! That's an experience I'd recommend placing on anyone's bucket list, and since you'd be in the area, stop by and tour the Corvette Museum in Bowling Green. The cars on display in the museum are like eye candy for a car fanatic. I've always admired and wanted a 'Vette, so I fulfilled that desire in 2013 when I purchased a Grand Sport.

On our way back from the derby, we stopped in Memphis, Tennessee, and toured the Lorraine Motel. Humbling doesn't describe how one might feel standing on the site of yet another American tragedy. While in Memphis, we tried what Tennesseans claim to be world-class barbecue. Nah! It's not that good compared to some backyard Texas barbecue. We also strolled Beal Street. This trip stirred a desire to travel and see the things one reads about or sees on television.

After that first trip, we started to take yearly road trips with two very special friends I call Big Fella and Boss Lady. Our first trip together was to the West Coast, stopping in Phoenix, Arizona, before making it to San Rafael,

California. Across the bay over the Golden Gate Bridge and into San Francisco, we dined along Fisherman's Warf and traveled down Lombard, the most crooked street in the world. While in California, we went to see the big tree just up the coast in Muir Woods. The drive up the mountain to where the trees are is still being talked about amongst us because the Boss Lady and Ernestine screamed all the way up and back down. Really, I don't blame them because the route went winding almost straight up and back down the mountain without any guard rails. If you looked out the window, you'd see where you would land if you didn't pay attention.

The Grand Canyon was next on our itinerary. Any picture you see of the canyon doesn't compare to seeing it with your own eyes. Only then you'll appreciate its breathtaking beauty. And if you have the nerve, stand along the rim and look down. On another road trip, we ended up in Yellowstone National Park, where we witnessed Old Faithful erupt!

Before getting there, we stopped in Cody, Wyoming, and visited Mount Rushmore and Chief Crazy Horse Monument. On our way back, we stopped in Colorado to tour the Garden of the Gods, drive up Lookout Mountain, and make the trip up Pike's Peak. One must possess some big ums because the ride up Pike's Peak to the summit is not for the weak-hearted. It's really scary! At over 14,000 feet above ground level, the view is breathtaking.

Travel and life as we knew it was placed on pause when my mother-in-law, Mrs. Bernice Johnson, well into her 80s, experienced a fall in late 2016 while visiting Dallas. Her fall resulted in her being hospitalized with a fracture to her leg. Ernestine and I made trips to Dallas for weeks, checking on her mom. We spent Christmas with her that year in Dallas, but the injury to her leg and the tension within the family did not help. Her condition worsened. Yet, despite her illness, she wanted to come home. Arrangements were made for her release, and she was transported home. Shortly after returning home, Mom transitioned from this world on January 3, 2017, at the golden age of 88. It often appears that if it isn't one thing, it's another. The following Thursday, January 6, 2017, the news came that GG had passed at age 86. If that wasn't enough, on January 8, 2017, Sister's only child, Rechelle, passed at age 50. To say that times were stressful is an understatement. Having three deaths in the family in such short order will test anyone's metal and devastate the family. If you've experienced the loss of a loved one, you know death can cause friction amongst family members in many areas.

Through it all and with God's hands on the wheel, we made it through a really tough time. Because no one will know the time or when death will occur, without a doubt, Rechelle's death was shocking. By then, Sister was struggling with dementia and other serious health issues. One would think with her age and health concerns…you know…we thought we'd receive a call about her. Nonetheless, Rechelle battled her own issues, and as a family, we made several attempts to get her the help she needed, but without success. Her death was recorded as having been caused by chronic ethanolism. After her death, Sister could not live alone while coping with the loss of a child and her medical history, so I brought her to live with me.

No one can imagine the difficulties a person will face when caring for someone with dementia until it happens to your family member. But, I remembered that Sister gave me a place to live as I found my way and never complained, so I felt obligated to her with whatever she needed.

In the meantime, we needed to make funeral arrangements for her daughter, but no local family members assisted with handling Rechelle's arrangements. It appears as though in every family, there's always one person everyone expects to handle everything. Now that I had Sister with me, I was occupied with her immediate care, financial obligations, and learning about her medical concerns and doctor's care. To figure out who and where her physicians were and her appointment schedule, to say the least, took time. I never knew one person could be on so many prescription meds. Moreover, having an elderly relative live in a home with stairs creates a safety concern. Fearing a fall, she demanded my constant attention as she would go searching for and asking for Rechelle. Reluctantly, after many discussions and prayer, the family agreed it would be in Sister's best interest (safety-wise) to have professionals care for her. Boy! We were shocked to learn the costs associated with having a relative living in a personal care facility!

With my hands full, our brother-in-law took the lead and, with Irene, worked to find a facility we would approve of and could afford. They researched and visited several facilities before we found the one we chose. Through prayer and God's guidance, we were led to a home we comfortably felt would care for her. We knew God had answered our prayers because the place was a facility with a home-like environment and a professional staff. It was also affordable and CLEAN!

After Sister transitioned to the facility, I made regular trips to her house to check on the property and to keep up the exterior maintenance. Eventually, we decided to lease the property so it could be occupied, and the amount charged would help supplement her healthcare costs. I will advise anyone to do their homework and vet potential tenants before signing a lease. One should also be cautious before leasing property to someone you know or a relative because it never turns out well. Since Sister would never be able to return to live there, we eventually decided to list her property for sale. The decision to sell made practical sense and the tenant was informed of our future plans upfront. After the sale became final, it almost took a court filing before the tenant honored the terms of the lease and vacated the property. Although no court action occurred, it required a law enforcement visit before the tenant honored the terms. The proceeds from the sale of the house (after the loan was satisfied) were deposited into her bank account to be used for her care.

For the next four years, I juggled the responsibility of caring for my family and remaining committed to my promise to Mr. Henry. Mrs. Marsh and I visited Sister on Sunday afternoons at the care facility. I accepted what I was doing as my purpose in life; however, it had a toll on vehicles and myself. Needless to say, I never lost focus that all things are possible with God as your guiding light. Even though my responsibilities were always my first priority, we still found time for a road trip or cruise to relax our minds. I would like to forget the trips to Las Vegas. Here again, I knew better, but those machines will let you feed them and never get full! I would recommend visiting Hover Dam instead if you're in the area.

It's a fascinating feat of engineering.

The cruises we took were great as we visited many places. Many of the places brought to reality that we take so much for granted. To witness how many make very little and are just as happy only highlighted how we take so many things for granted. As we traveled on our road trips, we gained an educational perspective regarding that area and had tons of fun. On one trip, we visited the southern states of Mississippi, Alabama, Georgia, the Carolinas, and Virginia. If a person wishes to gain a perspective of what life was like for Blacks in the South, visit the museum in Montgomery, Alabama, where the clothing enslaved people wore for their hanging is on display. You will also see the body parts of slaves that whites took as souvenirs.

You will never get the whole story from visiting a museum, for there is so much intended to never be openly told. Herein, we are responsible for insisting that our kids get excited about learning everything they can about Black history. The information is available but requires a desire to learn.

Following a short visit along Myrtle Beach and a stop in Virginia, we spent the next day in Washington, D.C., strolling the Mall while visiting many of the monuments. One day does not allow enough time to take in all the sites, for there's so much to take in. Very little is taught or written about the part slaves had in constructing many of the buildings and monuments along the plaza. Still, it's another part of history intended to be left untold. For me, I left feeling proud of my heritage. Before reaching our next destination, New York—The Big Apple—we stopped along the Hudson River on the New Jersey side, taking a tour of Ellis Island. Looking up at Lady Liberty scratched off an item on the old bucket list. Standing along the Hudson, staring across at New York's skyline, should impress anyone. We really wanted to visit the site where the Twin Towers once stood, but time just didn't allow. We eventually made it to Niagara Falls, another bucket list item for me and our turn-around destination before heading home.

While away, we were aware that Hurricane Harvey was wreaking havoc in the Houston area, but we could only watch the news reports covering what was happening. Here, too, is a time when one must have unwavering faith that God's will shall be done and trust His protective hands. We eventually returned home and found all to be well. That particular trip logged over 4,200 miles, traveling through fifteen states.

After returning home, I again focused on Hazel and Sister's needs. For Sister, every day is unique because having dementia each day is different. If she needed something, the staff would call, and I would deliver what was requested. With each day presenting a different challenge, I begin the day being thankful for being able to see that day and accepting whatever God has planned for me. Routinely, I have to shop for Hazel's needs, pick up prescriptions, and see that she has a healthy meal. More so, she simply needed someone to talk with. Her days are rather simple. She gets up early and has breakfast cereal. After breakfast and taking her meds, she turns on the television. She then expects me to know about everything she sees on television. She'll say, "Little Boy, did you see it?"

Most of the time, I wouldn't worry about Sister's routine care for the staff became like family members. We keep a good supply of personal items, snacks, and puzzle books for her. The staff looks after Sister as if she were family. We didn't realize it initially, but I don't think we could have found a better facility. When I wasn't tending to things regarding Sister or Hazel, I tried to get in a little fishing with my friend Mr. Breedlove. Everybody calls him Ray, but his birth name is Ernest. He's enjoying life in his 80s and lives in Washington County. He likes to fish just as I do and looks forward to my visits. Also, he still eagerly awaits deer season, and there is a lot of "smack talking" about who got the biggest deer that year. He normally misses as many as he hits but will tell you, "I got me a shot."

Chapter Twelve

Coronavirus

It's never safe to assume that nothing will surprise you because you have been around for years. However, if we believe what is told to us in the Bible, we shouldn't be surprised. Remember, scripture advises us that nothing is new. I believe we have gotten so far removed or do not know about the word of God that we can't see or adhere to the constant reminders happening all around us. Near the end of 2019, a coronavirus, Covid-19, surfaced and would impact the world forever. The virus made its appearance in the U.S. in early 2020, and the "powers that be" downplayed its effects.

The pandemic caused unimaginable illnesses and deaths, shutting everything down, and people struggled with all the changes it caused. The fear of contracting the virus and its effect on people was frightening. The everyday things we took for granted were no longer routine. Food items, toilet paper, cleaning supplies, Lysol, and hand sanitizers were no longer on store shelves...if the store was open. Individuals had to adjust to working from home, virtual learning, social distancing, worship via social networks, and learning to quarantine at home with family. The facility where Sister lived went into lockdown, not letting anyone in or out. I communicated by telephone with the staff, inquiring about her condition, and dropped off any needed items. They did an outstanding job, and, it goes without saying, times were still trying. Hazel still required attention, and contracting the virus was always on my mind. I did all that the professionals recommended, trying to protect myself. Ernestine was now working from home, so bringing the virus home was always a concern. With God's protective hands, masks, and hand sanitizers, we managed to remain safe until a vaccine was approved. Even then, life remained different, and no one could lower their guard. Being fully vaccinated did not prevent you from being infected, but it did relieve some of the stress because we knew the effects wouldn't be as bad.

Covid-19 took a toll on society, and many lost their lives due to the advice of those in charge. If dealing with the virus wasn't enough, the pandemic happened during a presidential election. Things don't just happen. They are allowed to occur to remind us of who's really in charge. Just as Barack Obama was elected president in 2008, it was no coincidence that Donald Trump was elected president in 2016. We thought things would be different after electing a Black president, but Donald brought everything to reality and showed us that racism is still alive and well. We were also reminded that bigotry still resides in plain sight in America. Things became crystal clear when the 2020 presidential candidates started their campaigns. I stayed glued to the television in my spare time, watching the impeachment hearings and campaign debates. What happened during the 2020 campaign season and following the defeat of the current president occupied the nation.

Prior to the inauguration of the next president, what happened on January 6, 2021, in my mind, compares to the events of November 22, 1963, and those of 9/11. I couldn't believe what was shown on live television with no attempts to shut down an insurrection! The participants were allowed to do as they pleased. They destroyed property, killed, and injured, while the person in the White House did nothing. If it had been us (you know), the response would have been different. It's something I will never forget. Somehow, the country survived, and the new president, Joseph Biden, was sworn in, and the country transitioned to another administration. Combined with the virus and the turmoil it created, the political climate and all the false information drove some to do all sorts of stupid things.

All that happened on January 6 will forever impact this nation's future. Although many people lined up to be vaccinated, others resisted the election results and refused to be vaccinated, so the turmoil continued. Things started to look a little brighter after the vaccine, and the powers that be started to loosen things up a bit. Hazel was first to be vaccinated, followed by Ernestine, with me getting vaccinated last. The facility where Sister lived arranged to have her vaccinated. Many businesses started to regain patrons, and the number of people allowed to attend in-person worship increased. The facility where Sister lived also started to allow limited visits to their facility. I was looking forward to seeing Sister again after hearing the update, but that wasn't to be. Around 10:00pm on March 13, 2021, I received a phone call reporting Sister was being transported to a hospital.

The staff advised me that she was having difficulty breathing. Shortness of breath at times was nothing new because Sister suffered from chronic obstructive pulmonary disease (COPD) and asthma. The staff would administer her medications, and up to that point, the meds helped manage her conditions. I obtained the location of the hospital, and Ernestine and I immediately drove there. Having left home thinking this would be another one of her many episodes that occurred at various times, I wasn't prepared for the news I got once the doctor came out to speak with me. This time, God saw fit to call Sister to judgment, and at 10:39 that night, she was pronounced dead. No one wants to hear news of a loved one passing, but this was like a slap to the face. After gathering myself, I realized that although the news hurt and I would miss Sister, her troubles were now over. As we drove back home, I contacted my siblings to inform them of our loss. I don't know what their immediate reactions were, but I believe they, too, were relieved to know she would no longer be sick.

As with any death, preparing for a funeral and her homegoing celebration were the next matters to be attended to. Once again, no one stood up to say they would handle this or that matter. Old Nelson drew the short straw. After her daughter's death, I purchased a pre-need burial packet for Sister using money from the sale of her house. Still, there is so much to be resolved following a death. There are outstanding obligations, closing utilities, Social Security, employee benefits notifications, and other claims against the estate. Because I had made earlier preparations, some matters were already handled. Having spent so much time with her during our earlier and later years and considering all she had done for us, I wanted to eulogize my sister at her homegoing celebration. I've had many opportunities to speak in front of an audience while employed and was comfortable doing so, but no one can imagine how difficult this can be unless you have stood to speak in honor of a loved one. With prayer, the support of the family, and God's steady hand, I was able to stand in honor of our Sister. In her heyday, she was a force to be reckoned with. If you wanted a spirited discussion, speak negatively about her beloved Cowboys. She would literally fight you about 'Them Boys'. With her fighting spirit, she had a caring and giving heart that never stopped giving to her family. After everything was done and her remains were laid to rest, I thought I would have time to relax and enjoy my golden years.

Still, there were things that had to be handled. Because of the virus's impact on everything, it took seven months to receive and have a monument placed at her grave site.

I continue to be thankful for each day I have the privilege to say, "good morning." After a good cup of Folgers, I start the day as I did the day before. At a certain stage in life, it's a little late for long-term plans because those should have been made and put into place during your earlier years. Truth be told, every breath is a gift, from your first to the last one taken. So prepare daily. The only certainty is you have lived your yesteryears, and yesterday is gone. Today is the most important day of your life, so make the most of every moment because the next may not come for you or the ones you may need to say "I love you" or ask for forgiveness.

I pray I'm blessed to hang around for a few more hunting seasons, do some more fishing, and have time to really appreciate life. I haven't mentioned this, but Ernestine has threatened to evict me if I come home with another mounted deer head. I have an expensive habit of hunting whitetail deer or searching for largemouth bass, just as I chased pretty little things back in the day. The only thing that remains from my days of chasing pretty little things are memories of the dumb stuff I did. Today, I reflect on the time spent at deer camp, in the woods, or on a lake. Today, there's nothing like looking at a mount on the wall

and reflecting on the occasion a particular deer showed up or reliving the thrill of a largemouth bass attacking my lure.

Being born into poverty with nothing but the name I was given to where I am today…God has truly blessed my life. I still have to visit Hazel daily just to see that things are well with her. I spend the rest of my time aggravating Ernestine, listening to music, or working on my do-nothing list. Oh! By the way, we were blessed with a new grandbaby. Nelson Dwayne and Nikki gave him a name I can't pronounce. What Black Southern Baptist family names a child Nasir? I'll just call him "No Sir." Altogether, we have five grandbabies: Keana, Al-Eyah, Fariah, Kaysen, and No Sir. And two grand dogs.

Without regrets, I have had many ups and downs, made mistakes, had disappointments, and had many regrets, but I've received many blessings. All that occurred molded me into who and where I am today. I have been blessed with God's promise of three scores and ten, and I thank Him for every moment.

I thank God for every moment; if not for His presence, I know things would have been different. I adopted the belief long ago that I would determine my future and be accountable for every decision I made. I would not allow anyone to influence which road I took or any decision I would make. I never got too worked up about what people thought or said about me. If you ask my opinion on a matter, I'll share what I think. If my opinion differs, we simply disagree. I have little tolerance for disrespect and wasn't built to back down. There are times when a person will approach you or ask a question in a way to receive the kind of response they want. There's nothing wrong with being different but be prepared for the criticism you'll receive. You will never satisfy everyone, so don't try.

I find peace in knowing I can talk with the Master about everything, anytime, and if in good faith, wait and watch. I knew that if I followed what God commanded in Exodus 20: 2-17 and Deuteronomy 5:6-21 and sought His guidance in prayer, I would be alright. There are many who pray to God and make the hair on the back of the neck rise. I get satisfaction in knowing God listens to everyone, even a country bumpkin like me. If you are sincere as you talk with God, He will listen to you. I believe that my pleas for forgiveness have been heard. If it's His will and I'm granted additional years beyond His promise, it will be satisfying to hear my kids tell theirs, "I tried that on Daddy. It didn't work then, and it won't work now."

Chapter Thirteen

A Good Life…Greater Comes Later

Many people impacted my life and influenced how it turned out, and I am thankful. Even though my biological daddy was absent, I was blessed to have a mother who took little to nothing and thanked God for that. Mama endured some unbelievable times but never complained and never stopped believing God would make a way. She instilled in all her kids the value of what a belief in God meant in one's life. She taught us to stand up for what we believe, always tell the truth, don't steal, and treat others with respect. Life struggles didn't keep her from believing that God would never leave her.

After Mama passed, I had a mother-in-law who had those same values and faith in God. Even though I became her son-in-law in 1981, she always said I was like a son to her. She would remind anyone that God never sleeps and that she would watch, fight, and pray. She would also say,

"Boy, you never know who might have to bring you a glass of water."

She was a graceful lady with a giving heart. To show her love for me, she would say,

"Come here, boy, and let me maul your head."

After she passed, Hazel took over as matriarch and said Mama had given her permission to finish raising me. She also came up with little to nothing but never gave up on believing God would make a way. She is another graceful lady with a giving heart who, if crossed, would show a side you didn't know she had and often threatened me with a belt. Three amazing women who, throughout their lives, endured many tough times but showed me what faith in God can do. Even still, never underestimate the impact a man being in the home will have on raising a boy to become a man. My daddy failed as a father but left me many examples of what not to do. Fellas, hang in there, and don't fail as a father.

I was given a mate who is owed so much credit for how my life turned out. We have known one another for many years and have been united for forty-plus. Anyone who'd put up with my shit for that many years had to have meant what the preacher told her to say. Many are eager to display their wealth, societal status, and everything they amassed. I never wanted notoriety or something to be named after me. For her to stand by me through it all, overlook my faults, and mean the vows she took in October 1981, she is my superstar. She made a man out of "Mr. Good Time Charlie."

We began our journey together with just enough to satisfy the necessities to get by. With my Father's blessings, we no longer fret about not having enough to satisfy the necessities. Nowadays, we are blessed to enjoy more than enough. You see, wine gets better with age, but one must have faith and be willing to wait. I will admit that I did not follow the script as I should have and was out-of-bound at times, but I must have done a few things right because God overlooked my many flaws and allowed for some amazing things to happen. Just as Ernestine supported my career, I always encouraged her in whatever she decided to pursue. After she left the retail field in the late 90s and entered the healthcare profession, she is now the regional manager for the southwest region of a major health management company. Now that the kids are gone, she no longer has to drive a "Mommy Mobile." She now rolls in a nice car.

Earlier, I mentioned that I brought my country swag to H-town. Don't blame me for how I was raised or what I say or do. I'm a country boy. I'm proud of where and how I was raised, and my love of country living forever remains in my heart. Most times, while riding around, I'm tuned to country music. I listen to all genres of music, but country is my go-to choice.

I won't try to influence anyone, for you make your own decisions. However, I suggest you think about what your life will say about you when you leave. My life while here and the legacy I leave are important to me. I believe a person's life can be judged by the legacy left. I pray my examples, efforts, and instructions will have established a sound foundation for my children, and hopefully, they will carry my last name forward with pride. Your parents and your name are the only things you are given; you must work to achieve the rest. Work for what you get, manage your earnings wisely, and think about the legacy you leave. It would be wise not to leave a financial strain on your family, so prepare for the inevitable because death is the price we all pay for living. Life insurance at an early age can help to build wealth for future generations. We all will be better off if we initiate things early in life that will result in generational wealth for those carrying your family's name forward. Preparing your last will and testament will help mitigate turmoil among family members. Lastly, if you don't want folks stretching the truth at your homegoing celebration, prepare it beforehand. Who best knows the truth but you and God?

Talk with your kids about your struggles and those of your forefathers so they know the whole story of what it took for them to live as they do. Impress upon them that knowledge is the key to success because a fool and money don't belong together. The Bible teaches about leaving an inheritance to those worthy, but place stipulations so they show themselves worthy. If our kids are not knowledgeable about God's words, "By the sweat of your brow, you will eat your food," how can they know? I take that to mean you must work for what you get and not wait for someone to die to leave you something. If someone chooses to take the road to nowhere and become involved with dumb stuff or associate with people living for the moment, have the courage to omit the unworthy. Please be mindful that we all have made dumb mistakes, so be conscious of the decisions you make.

I've shared a lot about myself and made a few suggestions for your consideration. Please take my suggestions for their worth to you. You should also know some things will remain between me and God. I hope sharing my story will serve to motivate someone to believe that just because you are born into a certain situation, you shouldn't allow that to prevent you from achieving the goals you set. I was neither the sharpest tool in the shed nor smarter than the average Joe. I don't believe a person isn't smart because they are not afraid to challenge another on a subject and, instead, stand on the principles instilled within them. I further believe if you are afraid of offending someone by standing on the truth, you are doing both a disservice. I was not fortunate to continue my education beyond high school, but I had a willingness to learn and work for what I wanted. The values Mama instilled and my belief that all things are possible by trusting God with whatever and wherever he leads, you too can be successful. I never begrudge anyone for what they do or have. There's enough for everyone. I am the result of what God can do. Don't look to anyone to give you anything or cut corners. Put forth the effort and wait for your blessings. You'll understand it by and by. And don't do the dumb things I did.

The man known as Nelson will, at some point, be no more and remain only in the memory of those left. Whatever family that remains has been made aware of my desires. They would have preferred not to have these conversations, but being informed prevents turmoil when the inevitable occurs. Aside from giving thanks daily, I further pray that my last moment finds me pleasing Him.

When my appointed time arrives, you shouldn't spend time worrying about my salvation. I believe I got that fixed. You should make sure of your salvation so you might receive what has been prepared for you.

Oh! By the way, if you are ever in Washington County, Texas, please take the time and go visit Washington-on-the-Brazos State Park.

The park's museum houses lots of ancestry records and memorabilia concerning the role the site played in the fight for Texas's independence from Mexico. It also details what life in early-day Texas was like. But please, don't lose focus on the real reason why Texas fought for its independence from Mexico. You'll find the trip educational, and I believe you will be pleasantly surprised at all the park offers. Take your children.

As for now, I'll have to wait to see if tomorrow will come for me. For now, that's my story.

9 798218 289416